J. Krishnamurti

Great Liberator or Failed Messiah?

J. Krishnamurti

Great Liberator or Failed Messiah?

LUIS S.R. VAS

MOTILAL BANARSIDASS PUBILISHERS
PRIVATE LIMITED • DELHI

First Indian Edition: Delhi, 2004

ISBN: 81-208-2050-9 (Cloth)
ISBN: 81-208-2051-7 (Paper)

MOTILAL BANARSIDASS
41 U.A. Bungalow Road, Jawahar Nagar, Delhi 110 007
8 Mahalaxmi Chamber, 22 Bhulabhai Desai Road, Mumbai 400 026
236, 9th Main III Block, Jayanagar, Bangalore 560 011
120 Royapettah High Road, Mylapore, Chennai 600 004
Sanas Plaza, 1302 Baji Rao Road, Pune 411 002
8 Camac Street, Kolkata 700 017
Ashok Rajpath, Patna 800 004
Chowk, Varanasi 221 001

Printed in India
BY JAINENDRA PRAKASH JAIN AT SHRI JAINENDRA PRESS,
A-45 NARAINA, PHASE-I, NEW DELHI 110 028
AND PUBLISHED BY NARENDRA PRAKASH JAIN FOR
MOTILAL BANARSIDASS PUBLISHERS PRIVATE LIMITED,
BUNGALOW ROAD, DELHI 110 007

CONTENTS

Introduction

The Theosophical Society (TS) was founded in 1875 by Madame H.P. Blavatsky and Colonel H.S. Olcott to preserve and promote the world's spiritual heritage. Many of its leaders, however, seemed to be more fascinated with its occult, esoteric—some would say, invented — aspects than with what others would consider real spirituality as indicated by Madame Blavatsky's book *The Secret Doctrine.* As the attraction of eastern religions for the theosophists seemed to gather momentum, it was decided to shift the headquarters of the TS from the West to Adyar, Madras, India in 1882. A year later, Charles Leadbeater, who was to play a crucial role in Krishnamurti's life, joined the TS. In 1889, Mrs. Annie Besant, who would be the successor to Blavatsky followed suit. The same year Blavatsky announced that the purpose of Theosophy was to prepare humanity for the coming of Lord Maitreya, World Teacher, for the Age of Aquarius.

On May 12, 1895, Jiddu Krishnamurti, eighth son of a high caste but impoverished Hindu Brahmin couple from Madanapalle, now in Andhra Pradesh, was born. His father, Jiddu Narayan, an employee of the Raj, was a member of the TS.

In 1906, Leadbeater was accused of paedophilia and forced to resign from the TS. A year later, on the death of Col. Olcott, the erstwhile President of the TS, Mrs. Besant was elected to the post.

The same year Krishnamurti's father had to take compulsory retirement from the government and volunteered to work for the TS at Adyar. On January 23, 1909, the Jiddu family moved to Madras and Krishnamurti began to attend the Penathoor Subramanyam High School at Mylapur, Madras. Later that year Leadbeater was readmitted to the TS. In May, he saw the 13-year-old Krishnamurti on the beach in Adyar and pronounced his aura to be completely free of selfishness and announced the Masters had chosen him to be the vehicle for the World Teacher. He was given the mystical name Alcyone. Krishnamurti would later recall about himself at this time: " The boy was affectionate, vacant, not intellectual, enjoyed athletic games. What is important in this is the vacant mind."

But 'vacant' was considered an understatement by some of his teachers. "The underfed, scrawny and dirty teenager" was considered dim-witted if not moronic by Ernest Wood, one of his teachers and author of books on Yoga. Leadbeater, for his part, was accused of "using Krishnamurti as a ruse to deflect attention from his past misdeeds and to give him an excuse to surround himself with small boys."

Irrespective of the charges, Leadbeater used to lock himself up with Krishnamurti in a room and report they were communing with the Masters. In such circumstances, on January 10, 1910, Krishnamurti said he had a vision of Lord Maitreya. (He would later have visions of other masters as well, until one day he walked through just such a vision of Master Kuthumi, whereupon the visions ceased. Ever since, Krishnamurti warned against induced visions).

Soon, Besant and Leadbeater had adopted Krishnamurti and his younger brother Nityananda, but their father claimed he "saw Leadbeater committing an unnatural offence with Krishnamurti" and threatened to take them back. He was repeatedly promised that Leadbeater would be kept away from them but the promise was broken. A book titled *At The Feet of the Masters* was published at around this time by the TS under the name of Alcyone, purporting to have been dictated by the Masters to Krishnamurti. Detractors claimed it had been dictated by Leadbeater. One of Krishnamurti's teachers later recalled seeing Krishnamurti laboriously writing the book. Krishnamurti himself later claimed not to remember writing it. He seemed to forget most crucial happenings of this time.

In 1911 'The Order of the Star in the East' was set up with Krishnamurti as its head to prepare humanity for the coming of the World Teacher. The two brothers were sent to England for further training in the new role. Their father sued Mrs. Besant demanding his sons back. He won in the lower courts but lost in the Privy Council which asked the boys to select their guardian: both selected Mrs. Besant.

Krishnamurti acquired a fondness for golf, motorbikes and expensive suits. He also took a fancy to detective thrillers which he would retain throughout his life as also to Wodehouse novels, whose expressions ("By Jove", "Old Boy") he would adopt. He repeatedly failed the entrance examinations of both Cambridge and London University, though Nityananda passed them with flying colours.

In 1922 Krishnamurti suffered from unusual but never diagnosed fainting spells which he termed "the process" which would recur throughout his life and would be attributed by some to the rising of the Kundalini. But these seizures were not disclosed to the public until the 1970s. From 1923 to 1931 he wrote some 60 mystical poems.

On November 23,1925, Nityananda unexpectedly died, depriving Krishnamurti of his last family bond and throwing him into a psychological crisis. The training for the coming of the World Teacher went on, however. In 1927, he wrote a letter to Leadbeater: "I know my destiny and my work. I know with certainty and knowledge of my own, that I am blending into the consciousness of the one Teacher and that He will completely fill me." A few months later he publicly announced: "I never said I am the World Teacher; but now that I feel I am with my Beloved, I say it." But, paradoxically, the man who was instrumental in picking Krishnamurti to fill the role of the new messiah was saying privately that "the Coming has gone wrong."

On August 2, 1929, at the annual camp of The Order of the Star in Ommen, Holland, Krishnamurti dissolved the Order, declaring that truth is a pathless land that cannot be approached through any organisation, and that his aim was to set man unconditionally free. He had already been complaining to Emily Lutyens, his surrogate mother, about his displeasure with the "circus" the TS had been building around him.

He now began to talk on his own behalf, warning against organisations claiming to lead others to truth. For decades he refused to let himself be photographed. Verbatim transcripts of his talks were published by Krishnamurti Writings Inc, run by a friend, D. Rajagopal. Rajagopal also edited Krishnamurti's series of books *Commentaries on Living* which were written at the behest of Aldous Huxley who wrote a foreword to an edited collection of his talks and dialogues, *The First and Last Freedom.* In all these writings Krishnamurti emphasised the importance of release from entrapment in the 'network of thought' through a perceptual process of attention, observation or 'choiceless awareness' which would release the true perception of reality without mediation of any authority, or guru.

Over the years Krishnamurti acquired many eminent friends like the physicist Dr. David Bohm and Dr. Allan Anderson, an eminent professor of religion, with whom he conducted book-length conversations which were published both as videos and in book form. Videos of his teachings were also made. He now appeared to lose his reluctance to be photographed and photographers had a field day recording his activities and publishing them in coffee table books like *Krisnamurti: The Years of A Thousand Suns* and *Krishnamurti: 100 Years.* A published diary, *Krishnamurti's Notebook,* now disclosed the periodic seizures which he termed "the process". Despite the wide dissemination of Krishnamurit's "teachings" there has been increasing doubt about how accessible they are to the public at large. Krishnamurti himself wondered whether he was a "freak" whose insight could not be communicated.

There was protracted disagreement with D. Rajagopal who denied Krishnamurti access to details of the running of Krishnamurti Writings Inc. It developed into lawsuits from 1968 to 1986 that were finally settled out of court. Krishnamurti Foundations were set up in America, England and India to spread Krishnamurti's teachings. Radha Burnier, who had worked for the Krishnamurti Foundation was elected president of the TS. Thereafter Krishnamurti was welcomed back into the TS' Adyar grounds. During his first visit he saw a large portrait of Leadbeater which hung there and muttered "Pax, pax" to it, as if to heal the decades-long rift.

In 1986, at the age of 91, Krishnamurti was diagnosed with cancer of the pancreas. He succumbed to it on February 17, 1986. After his death Rajagopal's daughter wrote a book charging Krishnamurti with having a 23-year affair with her mother, Rosalind Rajagopal, who was by this time already estranged from her husband.

Questions continue to be raised about Krishnamurti. How accessible are his teachings? Was he the World Teacher that the TS had promoted? Was there a rapprochement between him and the TS and on whose terms? And of course his teachings are constantly being evaluated. Although he railed against all organised religions, many religious leaders have praised his insights. Fr. Anthony de Mello, noted Jesuit writer, in his *The Way of Love*, virtually paraphrases Krishnamurti's teachings. Another Jesuit, Fr. Carlos Valles, has written admiringly about him. But, certainly, there have been detractors, too. Lama Anagarika Govinda has said: "Krishnamurti is the most conditioned man I know," implying that he has been reacting to his TS conditioning and not free from it, thus making the transmission of his insight ineffective. Others have pointed out that he suffers from a "no dog but I shall bark" syndrome, an arrogance of which he has been accusing others. Ken Wilber, a noted thinker, has charged him of being stuck midway on the spiritual ladder.

In this book I consider various assessments of Krishnamurti as well as charges against him, what might be the answers to them and, most important, how best to access his insight.

I acknowledge my indebtedness to all those who have been quoted in this book. Their names and sources are mentioned in the text.

LUIS S.R. VAS
vasluis@hotmail.com

Legacy

In death as in life there was only emptiness, wrote the author of an article which appeared in the Express Magazine of March 16, 1986, a month after Krishnamurti's death assessing Krishnamurti's legacy. "A framed portrait of J. Krishnamurti in profile, a perfectly chiselled, Roman Emperor's profile, formed the focal point at the far end of the vast airy room at Vasant Vihar, Madras where he used to stay. The floor coverings stretch across the room like the waves of the sea lapping the feet of a single sofa that rose with the dignity of a mountain in a Japanese painting. Placed on a small low table in the direction of the photograph was a vase of deep lotus blooms, heads closed bowing as if in sorrow. J. Krishnamurti was dead."

The article goes on with the description of the scene: "The guardian angels who had protected him against the stares or questions of the curious during his lifetime, now stood at the door with renewed zeal. Barring entry with the traditional gleaming swords. No interviews, no messages, no guided tours into Krishnamurti land. A silver urn containing his mortal remains had been placed in the garden under the trees he had loved so well. A solitary personal attendant stood guard at a discreet distance as people came to pay their respects in silence. A few flowers decorated the urn on a small raised mud platform. Nothing vulgar of course—a garland of small jasmine buds, parijath blooms, with their orange stems upturned, the inner white core of a banana plant stem carved into lotus forms floating in small circles of water set into the four corners of the platform. The austere beauty of the Krishnamurti mystique was alive and well."

The author's mind goes back to "the dry tones of a typical Krishnamurti lecture grazing across the minds of his audience: 'Do you understand me? Are we going through this together? Is the speaker making himself understood? Or is it all going above your heads?' And then the agonizing silences. The silences were important. They were not the structured periods of meditation where a crowd might be outwardly quiet, but chattering mentally. These silences were tense moments when time stood still. All the attention was focused on the neat exquisitely dressed figure holding back a pale raw silk gold sleeve with utmost seriousness. A Krishnamurti audience prided itself on being above the average intellectually. If you confessed by chance that you did not, could not understand him, there were the usual pained smiles reserved for the mentally deficient. Yet many people would recognize themselves in the questioner who confessed, 'I hear those words but I can't really see what you are driving at.'"

To find out what Krishnamurti was driving at, the author approaches Rohit Mehta, Director, School of Wisdom, Theosophical Society. "What Krishnaji is trying to bring about is a shift in consciousness. In the normal course of our lives we are stuck at a particular point of consciousness. He wants to bring about a psychological mutation so that from a successive consciousness we can come to a simultaneous consciousness," says Mehta. Giving a series of lectures in the freshness of the tranquil green heart of the Theosophical Society, he clarifies the simplest doubts that arise in the minds of many people. He deals with the problem of language.

"How does the mystic communicate his experience? When there is a spiritual experience of such intensity, a mystic completely destroys the usual patterns of expression and brings about a fresh pattern of expression. He translates the spiritual experience using the language that is available. Krishnaji gives a completely new meaning to the pattern of language that was existing because of the tremendous pressure of the mystical experience but that experience cannot be conveyed through a consistent pattern of language, words that had meant something yesterday may not mean the same thing today. Which is why when he is talking we feel it is so simple, but when we come out there is nothing to which we can hold on." It is because of this that any translation or interpretation can distort the impact. One dares not call it a message. "No translation can contain that livingness or touch even a little bit of the consciousness of that which speaks," says Mehta.

At the same time Mehta asserts that "the brilliant teaching which is a precious gift of a unique individual to humanity, must be preserved." When it is pointed out that the books, cassettes, and lectures might then be a contradiction of the purity of such an approach he puts the question in a proper perspective: "the books, cassettes, etc, are road signs, a finger that points to the way. If there is no communication what are we to do? The difficulty arises when people cling to the finger and forget the way."

Radha Burnier, President of the Theosophical Society, puts the question of the continuity of Krishnamurti's teachings in another way. "What Krishnaji tried to do was to shake people out of a sense of complacency — the satisfaction or psychological comfort that might be derived from clinging on to the idea of a God or security, or certain fixed habits of thought that might fetter a person. He was such a force, he made you question everything, question what you say. Question what you hear. Even his own words. 'Use me as a mirror,' he would say, 'to question yourself. Don't be influenced by anyone, not even me. I am nobody.' This is probably why he used to be so insistent that there should be no cult built around him. Along with the questioning he also said, 'observe everything, listen to everything'. In this state of enhanced sensitivity you will begin to see that everywhere there is a message. Something is speaking."

As Burnier spoke the image of a remote seer confronting

a faceless audience with abstract truths appeared to fade. "He was so shy, so sensitive about meeting people," Burnier said, "that he could not accept the adulation that people felt for him." She recalls a time when, walking on the smooth stretch of sand on the deserted beach at the Theosophical Society, a woman who had caught sight of him fell at his feet. In the same moment Krishnaji had bent down and taking her hands in his had asked, 'Amma, how are you?' "There was such an outpouring of love and tenderness in that moment of contact that it seemed to radiate from him. On another occasion a little fisherboy appeared and started begging. Krishnaji had nothing in his hand but as you know he was always beautifully dressed. There was always certain grace and dignity in everything he wore but at that moment he took out his waist coat and wrapping it around the fisherboy made him a gift of it."

There was, she says, an intense childlike wonder and excitement in the way Krishnaji looked forward to the walks along the Adyar beachfront. The sight of the water lapping the shore, the lazy grace of the slender white herons circling their way through the weeds, the thrill of discovering new shoots on a fence of thorns that had been erected along the edge of the backwaters, could trigger a deep joy. Some of these observations of nature, the author observes, may be seen in the volume of Krishnamurti's daily record of events made during the latter part of June 1961 and collected under the title *Krishnamurti's Notebook.*

"At one level they may be read as the detailed notes of a particularly intense lover of nature. As for instance a typical passage that reads: 'It was a beautiful, quiet evening; there was a breeze among the leaves and the aspen leaves were trembling and dancing. A tall straight stem of a plant, with a crown of white feathers, touched by a faint pink stood as a watcher by the mountain stream.' At another level they are mystical songs or simple exercises that sharpen the mind into new states of perception. They are lessons in developing the state of alert awareness, each moment appears to be created anew. Each instant promises the discovery of a new world. Perhaps it is the choiceless awareness that he talks about. As Rohit Mehta explains it, "choiceless awareness is a non-dual state when there is no entity that says, this is non-dual. The 'I' does not exist." Perhaps it is the "stopping of the world" that Don Juan talks of to Carlos Castaneda. If in the talks and dialogues Krishnamurti proves to be a relentless teacher who strips aways layer after layer of belief and thought, in the *Notebook* he is his most compassionate, gentle self. 'Shadows fill the earth, it was a morning for shadows, the little one and the big ones, the long lean ones and the fat satisfied ones, the squat homely ones and the joyful sprightly ones.'"

In this frame of reference, the article's author comments, the legend of Krishnamurti acquires a certain mythic quality. There is the sheer physical beauty of the man who would have been a god. The story of how the half boy, half man was "discovered" on the beach at Adyar by one of the leading lights of Theosophy and taken by Annie Besant to London (along with his younger brother Nitya) is told in fascinating detail by Mary Lutyens. Her mother, Emily Lutyens, a staunch follower of Annie Besant, and also wife to Edwin Lutyens, the inspired architect of imperial Delhi, was to become the foster mother to the young Krishnamurti. The transformation of the "undernourished scrawny" Brahmin boy into a young god batting his luminous eyes in the glare of adulatory worshippers was not without its tragic undertones. The father of the two boys was to bitterly regret the loss of his two sons and fight an unsuccessful battle for their custody. By this time Krishnamurti was already being tutored to talk, eat, dress, think, act like a potential candidate for a higher manifestation. His teeth were straightened out, he was taught how to polish his shoes till they shone like "chestnuts". Obviously it would not do if the chosen vehicle had bad teeth or found it painful to wear shoes.

These changes were, however, on a superficial plane. Ever since reaching Ojai Valley in California, Krishnamurti began experiencing strange symptoms of pain that would shoot up his spine or lodge in his head till he became unconscious. He was not, his biographer informs us, an epileptic nor under the influence of drugs. She can only describe the symptoms as "the process" that would go on for several years leaving the body more and more "tuned" or sensitive. His preceptors at the Theosophical Society, while aghast at the extreme torture that he suffered could only be pleased when in the course of a meeting at Adyar, talking under the branches of a great banyan tree he suddenly changed his tones from the third person to the first person and announced, "I come not to destroy but to build." Besant herself was to write, " we knew that the waiting period was over and the morning star had risen over the horizon." The World Teacher had arrived. It did not matter if, when he landed in New York to be faced with a battery of reporters, one of them should describe him as a "shy, badly frightened, nice looking young Hindu boy, slight in figure, with straight blue-black hair, soft brown eyes and drooping eyelashes." They did not know that soon the nice boy was going to shake the foundations of the Society that had created him and waited for him to mature through eighteen years of nurturing. During this time he had lost Nitya, his dearly beloved brother and the only link from his childhood years. Was it the psychological shock of his loss, for Nitya was also supposed to play a part in his chosen destiny, that finally led him to break away? Or was it the growing sense of disenchantment at being made to play the part of a "freak"? Whatever the reason or reasons, the speech he made in 1929 at Ommen camp rang out with a certain prophetic quality. "I maintain that truth is a pathless land and you cannot approach it by any path whatsoever, by any religion, by any sect. My only concern is to set man absolutely, unconditionally free. These words will always remain a vital part of the Krishnamurti legacy.

"Krishnamurty was only 34 years old. The major part of his life and life's work lay ahead of him during this time the great upheavals of the 20th century — World War II, the revolutions, the freedom movements, the awakening of the technological era and the nuclear age — were to take place. One criticism that is levelled against him is that he seemed to keep aloof from these events. One can only quote his words as a possible answer, 'we are concerned with bringing about in our lives a total revolution which has nothing to do with the structure of society as it is. On the contrary unless we understand the whole psychological structure of society of which we are a part, which we have put together for centuries, and are entirely free from that structure, there can be no psychological revolution and a revolution of that kind is absolutely essential.' Or yet again in a simpler form, 'we human beings as individuals are totally responsible for the state of the world.'"

The article goes on to refer to the schools set by Krishnamurti as a part of this responsibility. "The school at Madras is not as large as some of the others but it is an oasis of beauty. 'We are trying to give the children a global outlook,' says the teacher. They call her "Big Sister" and she cuddles the little ones with utmost affection. It is a long way indeed from the school Krishnamurti himself went to, where the teacher would beat him every day and send him out of the class to sit on the verandah until it was time for him to go home. But all schools have walls. This one is no exception. At the far end of the playing fields where the wall is particularly high and strong like a fortress a couple of street urchins are playing on the other side of the wall. It is a dead end, a secluded corner that carries a strong stench of sun baked excrement but none of the scrawny, undernourished boys appear to notice it. One of them climbs the wall catching the barbed wire fence that has been placed across the top of it. What does he see? Freedom? Love? Beauty? Or just the other side of the wall? Or perhaps these are just words and as Krishnamurti says in his *Notebook:* 'every word, thought, shapes the mind and without understanding every thought, mind becomes a slave to words and sorrow begins.'"

The legacy of J. Krishnamurti is that there is no legacy, the author of the article concludes. "In emptiness alone there can be creation."

But there is a literary legacy of J. Krishnamurti. The life of J. Krishnamurti has been much chronicled by several distinguished writers who had known him for years and intimately. Mary Lutyens, his official biographer, has written four volumes while Pupul Jayakar has concentrated more on the Indian episodes of his life, especially in the post-war era, by which time K was in his fifties and his teachings had acquired a greater depth and seriousness. To a vast number of Indians, his annual round of public talks, held nearly always in the cooler months, was the high point of their calendar. Beyond these biographies, however, the literature of J. Krishnamurti's teachings is vast and varied, and spread over nearly 60 years and 15 million words. From his early talks and discussions in the Twenties to his death in 1986, the officially recorded sources alone number over 2,600 occasions. Each represents a talk, a question-answer session with the audience, intensive discussions with groups of scholars and scientists or special dialogues with personalities in different fields of knowledge and inquiry.

Where does one begin reading Krishnamurti? Many would consider his *Commentaries on Living* in three volumes as the best start. Others would recommend beginning with *The First and Last Freedom* which has a foreword by Aldous Huxley. Still others would suggest *Freedom From The Known.* It is short, has been edited with great care by Mary Lutyens, is exquisitely simple and reveals the depths of his teachings.

"Most of us walk through life inattentively, reacting unthinkingly according to the environment in which we have been brought up, and such reactions create only further bondage ... but the moment you give your total attention to your conditioning, you will see that you are free from your past completely, that it falls away naturally".

Again, "have you ever noticed that when you respond

to something totally, with all your heart, there is very little memory? Anything that is the result of memory is old and therefore never free. Thought is never new ... (it) makes this thing which you have looked at with delight, old. There is no Time in the new".

"The observer is the observed," declares Krishnamurti and immediately pounces on the next obvious question that leaves many people initially disappointed. Do not ask how. That to him is a wrong question, one that would (logically, please note, not by some magical revelation) lead to yet another "thought-control" method engineered by thought itself. A prescription for failure, for further conflict and a cycle of entanglement in the "I".

The verbal resolution of this situation, which is offered, is variously worded but fundamentally rests on a "continuous, intelligent awareness" of everything both inside and outside of oneself.

The *Commentaries On Living* series was published in the Fifties and goes back to records kept during the middle period of his life. In three volumes, it is a lucid and accessible introduction to the Teachings, which is strongly recommended to anyone coming to them for the first time. The pieces are short, seldom more than three or four pages long. They begin with a brief, but vivid, description of nature or the immediate surroundings. This is followed by comments on the problems or questions posed by someone who happened to come to meet him; and end with a drawing together of the insight, from the particular to the general to the universal. These may take the form of musings of the havoc caused to human relationship by fear, jealousy, prejudice or anger, all of them leading one back to the divisive and fragmentary instrument of thought and "self" or a combination of images put together by it.

"Opposite the entrance to the fashionable club, a beggar was seated on the ground; he was covered with a filthy gunny sack, and his matted hair was full of dust. One evening there was gaiety at the club; it was lit up, and sparkling cars full of laughing people were driving in, tooting their horns. From the club-house came light music, loud and air filling. Many policemen were at the entrance, where a large crowd had gathered to watch the smartly dressed and well-fed people pass by in their cars. The beggar turned his back on all this. One man was offering him something to eat, and another a cigarette, but he silently refused both without making a movement. He was slowly dying, day-by-day, and the people passed by".

The personal writings — as distinct from edited transcripts of talks, discussions, interviews, dialogues and discussions — are a class apart. They provide a unique insight into the mind of a truly exceptional, yet ordinary, human being of the 20th Century. These are reflective and at times amusing, full of great depth and insight on the one hand and remarkably detailed descriptions of nature on the other.

In the last 25 years of his life, Krishnamurti employed, for short spells, the medium of a personal diary or notebook, which take one deeper and more into the subtle core of his teachings. They also offer a unique view of the extraordinary states of stillness, a meditative mind, of what he refers to as a Benediction and the "otherness".

"The earth was the colour of the sky; the hills, the green, ripening rice fields, the trees and the dry, sandy river-bed were the colour of the sky; every rock on the hills, the big boulders, were the clouds and they were the rocks. Heaven was the earth and the earth heaven; the setting sun had transformed everything. The sky was blazing fire, bursting in every streak of cloud, in every stone, in every blade of grass, in every grain of sand.

The sky was ablaze with green, purple, violet and indigo, with the fury of flame. Over that hill it was a vast sweep of purple and gold; over the southern hills a burning delicate green and fading blues; to the east there was a counter sunset as splendid in cardinal red and burnt ochre, magenta and fading violet. The counter sunset was exploding in splendour as in the west; a few clouds had gathered themselves around the setting sun and they were pure, smokeless fire, which would never die.

The vastness of this fire and its intensity penetrated everything and entered the earth. The earth was the heavens and the heavens the earth.

And everything was alive and bursting with colour and colour was god, not the god of man. The hills became transparent, every rock and boulder was without weight, floating in colour and distant hills were blue, the blue of all the seas and the sky of every clime. The ripening rice fields were intense pink and green, a stretch of immediate attention. And the road that crossed the valley was purple and white, so alive that it was one of the rays that raced across the sky. You were of that light, burning, furious, exploding, without shadow, without root and word. And as the sun went further down, every colour became more violent, more intense and you were completely lost, past all recalling. It was an evening that had no memory". (Krishnamurti's Notebook, pp.188-89, Rishi Valley, November 17, 1961, (c) KFI.)

In reading these one is struck by the acuity of observation as well as the sensitivity of the whole being. A bird in flight catching the sun's rays in its plumage, moonlight on a rippling river's surface, a squirrel on the verandah, a labourer working on the roadside, totally lost in what he is doing — nothing escapes the eye of total and unclouded observation.

Krishnamurti's journal and *Krishnamurti To Himself* are later volumes in the series, which too are worth seeking for the sheer power of the language alone.

"There is a tree by the river and we have been watching it day after day by several weeks when the sun is about to rise. As the sun rises slowly over the horizon, over the trees, this particular tree becomes all of a sudden golden. All the leaves are bright with life and as you watch it as the hours pass by, that tree whose name does not matter — what matters is that beautiful tree — an extraordinary quality seems to spread all over the land, over the river. And as the sun rises a little higher, the leaves begin to flutter, to dance. And each hour seems to give to that tree a different quality. Before the sun rises it has a sombre feeling, quiet, far away, full of dignity. And as the day begins, the leaves with the light on them dance and give it that peculiar feeling that one has of great beauty. By midday its shadow has deepened and you can sit there protected from the sun, never feeling lonely, with the tree as your companion. As you sit there, there is a relationship of a deep abiding security and a freedom that only trees can know. Towards the evening when the western skies are lit up by the setting sun, the tree gradually becomes sombre, dark, closing in on itself. The sky has become red, yellow, green, but the tree remains quiet, hidden, and is resting for the night. If you establish a relationship with it then you have relationship with mankind. You are responsible then for that tree and for the trees of the world. But if you have no relationship with the living things on this earth you may lose whatever relationship you have with humanity, with human beings.

We never look deeply into the quality of a tree; we never really touch it, feel its solidity, its rough bark, and hear the sound that is part of the tree. Not the sound of wind through the leaves, not the breeze of a morning that flutters the leaves, but its own sound, the sound of the trunk and the silent sound of the roots. You must be extraordinarily sensitive to hear the sound. This sound is not the noise of the world, not the noise of the chattering of the mind, not the vulgarity of human quarrels and human welfare, but sound as part of the universe."

Part of Krishnamurti's legacy has been his dialogues with various thinkers. For example the book *Questioning Krishnamurti* has thinkers like Huston Smith and Iris Murdoch interacting with him and challenging him.

Among those who dialogued with K was an Argentinian doctor, Dr. Ruben Feldman-Gonzalez. During his encounters with people many asked him to write of his dialogues with Krishnamurti, even knowing he would be retrieving them only from his memory since only a few had been recorded. So it was that he started to think of writing some of his memories down. Some other friends felt that it was unnecessary to write these memories since Krishnamurti had done such a beautiful work of exposition of life and truth for mankind with his own books, videos and audiotapes. Nevertheless he wrote them in the hope that anyone who reads them will feel the need to read Krishnamurti himself.

Thereafter Dr. Feldman-Gonzalez says he almost stopped reading, and, if he did, it was only to read "*Krishnamurti Journals*" or "Commentaries On Living" by Krishnamurti and "*Collected Works of Krishnamurti*" (17 volumes) (1933-1967).

"Political contradiction in Argentina was always high," Dr. Feldman-Gonzalez begins his account . "It came to one of its highest points, though, by the end of August 1972. During this time a group of leftist, guerrilla men and women were killed while in jail at Trelew-Argentina, and I was horrified to hear that one of them had been a friend of the family. I started to get phone calls prompting me to take sides in the armed struggle: 'If you are not for the left you are for the right', a man's voice had told me on the phone before he hung-up while I was taking care of a recently born baby in Villada, Argentina, on August 23, 1972."

The following day he went to Buenos Aires to get a visa to the USA (1972) because he thought that if man loses respect for life we are all at risk from each other. Only after two years he got a temporary visa to enter the US. Every Argentinian was suspicious then. He stopped over in Puerto Rico. There was a man there he wanted to meet: Enrique Biascoechea. He did meet him. He was dying. He had been a friend of Krishnamurti since age nine. He wrote a letter to Krishnamurti telling him that Dr. Feldman-Gonzàlez had left behind his parents, two baby sons, possessions, friends, profession, comfort, and status in order to travel to meet with him. That was in June 1974. Enrique Biascoechea died in November 1974.

After reaching the US the doctor soon found himself working 16 hours a day as a resident physician in Pennsylvania. He needed a dictionary to dictate his notes, he writes. Of the other eight hours of the day he spent four in the basement to study medicine in English to revalidate his license. He slept three or four hours a day and ate only once a day, taking coffee in the morning and again at lunchtime simply to keep himself awake. Sometimes he wondered how his body could bear so much abuse! He got letters from Argentina: "Misery. My family and my friends kept disappearing".

He had given up hope of meeting Krishnamurti when he got a letter from Mrs. Zimbalist, dated January 5, 1975 from Ojai, California telling him he had a personal interview with Krishnamurti on March 23 at 4 P.M. at the Huntington Hotel in San Francisco, California. Mrs. Zimbalist volunteered her time for Krishnamurti as a devoted secretary. She is the widow of the late Sam Zimbalist, producer of the film "Ben Hur".

At 4.00 PM on March 23, 1975 sharp he knocked on Krishnamurti's door. Mrs. Zimbalist did everything to make him feel comfortable. Krishnamurti came after five minutes. "I stood up from the armchair to shake his hand. He looked smaller than I expected him to be. He wore an old blue jacket. He sat in front of me with nothing in between the two chairs. Mrs. Zimbalist left silently. We sat there looking at each other. I will never be able to describe that moment when Krishnamurti was gazing at me. I felt at the same time all the love I had felt for my parents, my sons, my girlfriends, my friends (dead or alive)... There was long silence."

Krishnamurti said: Biascoechea says you are ready to work for the Foundation.

Ruben : I may not be wise or free enough for that.
Krishnamurti : You will.
Ruben : What would the work imply?
Krishnamurti : Publishing books, videos and tapes.

Ruben : That implies managing money.

Krishnamurti : Millions of dollars.

Ruben : That horrifies me. I'm not ready for that. I thought I would have to travel with you, type your lectures from recorded tapes.... things like that.

Krishnamurti : (Laughing) You can do more than that, Dr...

Ruben : My name is Ruben Ernesto Feldman-Gonzalez.

Krishnamurti : That's confusing, may I call you Dr. Gonzalez?

Ruben : Of course, but my real name is Anger.

Krishnamurti : (touching my left knee) Ah! I'm glad you don't wear a mask like so many that come to me pretending to be saints.

Ruben : I'm far from that. I feel a complete repugnance for the so-called political situation of Argentina, my country of birth, and even for the way my profession is practised. I'm a pediatric surgeon. I had started to study psychiatry (July 1974) in Pennsylvania to see why the world has gone so crazy.

Nevertheless I'm not impressed, the approach to treatment in psychiatry is conventional... standardized. I'll leave psychiatry too. I don't know what I will do.

Krishnamurti : Don't leave psychiatry. Change it.

Ruben : I never thought you would give me concrete advice like that. It sounds absurd though. Changing psychiatry sounds like changing the colour of the crickets of the world.

Krishnamurti : You have to change psychiatry.

Ruben : I wish I knew what you meant.

Krishnamurti : You have to meet Dr. David Bohm in London. Let's go there soon.

Ruben : I wish I could, perhaps if I get a loan.

Krishnamurti : No! Don't ask for a loan. You'll meet him soon anyway.

Ruben : I need to make changes. I have no peace. Friends have disappeared in Argentina. Everything seems so chaotic and corrupt....

Krishnamurti : (smiling) You need exercise (Krishnamurti touched the doctor's belly with the tip of his left index finger).

Ruben : I work 16 hours a day and then I have to sit to study for four hours a day before I go to sleep. All this to renew my medical license in the USA.

Krishnamurti : That's an excuse. Take care of yourself. You need exercise. You look like a bull.

Ruben : Sometimes I feel that I need to share my understanding with people around the world. What do you say to that?

Krishnamurti : You speak.

A very long silence followed. Dr. Feldman-Gonzalez had expected K to tell him to "stay put" and spend the rest of his life in silent meditation. With very few words he became the perfect mirror letting the doctor's contradictions emerge and be clearly seen.

K insisted: The Foundation in Puerto Rico has no head. I hope you will take it (he grabbed the doctor's left knee).

Ruben : Krishnaji, when I was with Biascoechea everything seemed so easy. Now I see I don't have the peace of mind, the right skills nor the freedom (the sons and two parents to feed) to dedicate myself sensibly to such an important and difficult task. It is certainly no picnic.

Krishnamurti : I hope you take it.

Another long silence followed. Krishnamurti discussed several items regarding the Foundation's translations, people like Salvado Sendra, Vimala Thakar, personal and ideological struggles within the Foundations, etc.

Ruben : I'm eager to meet Salvador and Vimala... but people from the Fourth Path are trying to mix what you say with what others have said and are quite willing to control the Foundations.

Krishnamurti : That has been going on all the time and not only with them. The Fourth Path is a path of violence which reinforces the ego and the wish to control life and its course. Do not touch it. The first insight is to drop everything non-essential for the total liberation of mankind.

Ruben : Now that you mention the non-essential.... Why did you allow the biography of yours written by Lutyens to be published? It's gossipy and superficial, and it may not be right selling "At the Feet of the Master" ... with your name on it.

Krishnamurti : Not my books.

Ruben : And they are making a profit.

Krishnamurti : It's not my business.

Ruben : How would you recommend your books to be read, and in what order?

Krishnamurti : Do not read them like a novel. Read slowly as if your life was in every word and every sentence. Start with the last one and then if there is an interest go backwards through the first one.

Ruben : Should we read all your books?

Krishnamurti : If you take a train in San Francisco to go to Los Angeles... would you get off in Santa Barbara?

They both laughed. One had to laugh very often in the company of Krishnamurti, the doctor comments. Today the order of the books would be: "*Ending of Time*"; "*The Awakening of Intelligence*"; "*Commentaries on Living*";

"*Journal*"; "*Freedom from the Known*", etc.; "*Collected Works*" (1933-67)

Ruben : Why don't you eat meat?

Krishnamurti : Pity.

The doctor had expected a longer lecture but that was all he said. Again a long silence. "The silence was alive, the silence of two alert friends seeing together the same thing at the same time."

K stood up and said. "Excuse me Dr. Gonzalez, I'll prepare some tea for you". At the kitchen in the big suite he whispered something to Mrs. Zimbalist who was sitting there.

He came back with a cup of tea. He said: "Tea of roses for you". Ruben sipped it, but didn't like it. He left it on the little table beside them.

Ruben : Can we talk about meditation?

Krishnamurti : Is there anything else?

Ruben : Well, the very word meditation is used by gurus of all kinds to make money, sell silly books, techniques, pillows, crystals, mantras, and incense.

Krishnamurti : I have been using the word for 50 years. I can't change it now. People will have to see I use the word with a different meaning. I do not use the word meditation with its traditional meaning!

Ruben : What about using the expression "Unitary Perception" instead.

Krishnamurti : You use it.

(Krishnamurti said he would not use the word meditation anymore during his last talk in England in 1985, ten years later.)

Krishnamurti : Why not live very simply? Call it meditation or Unitary Perception. Self protection and self aggrandizement through money making and success have to end in order to live simply. To live simply is to live intelligently, without an observer in observation. If you believe you have to go back to Argentina to be loyal to some concept of yours you are not simple. If you are angry you are not simple. If you are full of sorrow you can't love anyone. Can you be spontaneous and simply act with not too much planning?

Ruben : You are not saying I have to remain alone and live in poverty and silence.

Krishnamurti : Would that be simple? Would you be escaping from life? The consummation of truth is not to be successful or wealthy... but do you want complete truth? Look for success or money and you'll find frustration. Look for truth and you'll receive total peace of mind and joy. Will you be one of the few? Or will you continue being one of the many worshippers of money and success?

After a long silence, he said: "Dr. Gonzalez, your tea must be cold already, finish it!" The doctor didn't have the courage to say no and did finish it silently.

K said: "Let's meet tomorrow at eight A.M."

Krishnamurti went with him to the door, opened it for him and smiled lovingly saying: "Good bye".

Ruben : What noun should be applied to what you teach—"message", "gospel",...or what?

Krishnamurti : Call it "the teachings". Let's meet tomorrow at eight A.M., right here.

Dr. Feldman-Gonzalez spent the rest of the afternoon by himself in his room, which he had rented at the same hotel where Krishnamurti was staying. He says he felt like a Condor for the rest of the day.

He met Krishnamurti by chance in the lobby that evening. He walked with him for awhile. They saw a couple of very beautiful girls.

Ruben : "God, how beautiful they are".

Krishnamurti : "Only well fed".

Ruben : "Krishnaji, I felt like a Condor the whole afternoon, full of peace and joy and love. I think it's because I spent some time with you."

Krishnamurti : "For how long do you want to be infected?"

March 24, 1975 (Huntington Hotel, San Francisco, California)

Krishnamurti : Sorry, I made you wait. I was doing some Hatha Yoga.

Ruben : No problem. Thank you for receiving me again. I would like to discuss the fact that you are the instructor of the world (or the Second Coming).

Krishnamurti : You worry about the irrelevant.

Ruben : It is relevant for me, because if you are the Instructor of the World, then I want to be an apostle.

Krishnamurti : There are no more apostles, Dr. Gonzalez. It is of critical urgency that human beings change radically. They have to detach themselves from the content of mankind's consciousness, they have to live without touching the stream of growing vulgarity and violence. Egocentric activity has to end, the desire for profit, power and prestige. One needs to learn to live psychologically alone, that is to be content without depending on anybody or anything.

Ruben : That they detach themselves from the content of mankind's consciousness?... then, how does one live?

Krishnamurti : You don't become comatose, you don't enter into a drug or alcohol induced trance, you don't live in a state of hypnosis, nor asleep even while awake. You live in complete attention. Are you aware that observation is attention?

Ruben : Fundamental action.

Krishnamurti : Observation is action. To observe totally doesn't mean to be negligent nor socially indifferent. If you observe totally, each one of your actions changes in nature. You free yourself from the choking grip of traditional memory and you also start to think sanely and freely. So there is total observation and new thought and action.

(A long time is spent in silence)

Ruben : Are you greater than Jesus?

Krishnamurti : Do you want me to say "yes"?

Ruben : Tell me what do you think?

Krishnamurti : Mankind is not the same. In the last 2000 years there have been three wars every year in the world and there has been a consequent degradation of human beings, the son of humanity can not be the same.

Ruben : You are talking of the Son of Man (with capital letters) aren't you? You are talking of the Greek "uios tou antropon" (the son of man). Aren't you?

Krishnamurti : The son of humanity is today the son of a degraded mankind. Then... what do you do?

Ruben : I listen to Krishnamurti.

Krishnamurti : For how long?

Ruben : Until I understand and radical change occurs.

Krishnamurti : Be a light to yourself. Stop procrastination. Throw away the content of consciousness. There has to be pure consciousness, pure awareness, pure listening.

Ruben : When I asked you whether I could speak publicly you said, "you speak".

Krishnamurti : You speak. "That" is not only for you.

Ruben : Can you tell me more about talking to people about all this?

Krishnamurti : You talk and expect no-thing.

(LONG PAUSE) (In vital silence) Krishnamurti had said "no-thing", he had not said "nothing".

Krishnamurti : It's time for lunch Dr. Gonzalez.

March 25, 1975 (Hotel Huntington, San Francisco, California)

Krishnamurti : Good morning Dr. Gonzalez.

Ruben : Good morning.

Krishnamurti : I guess you have some questions, right?

Ruben : You told me two days ago that you'll never die in an aircraft, what is it that makes you feel protected?

Krishnamurti : That.

Ruben : O.K. Please, tell me about That (Or the Other).

Krishnamurti : You can see That in action, but you can't talk about it.

(LONG PAUSE) (In complete silence)

Ruben : You already know that some of my friends disappeared in Argentina. Sometimes I feel deep sorrow for Argentina and for the rest of the world. How come so much horror?

Krishnamurti : You can be free of all conditioning and then you'll be free of sorrow. When you are not an Argentinian anymore you'll be able to do more for mankind and even for Argentina. I was born in India. I had an English passport. When India declared its independence from England I asked for an Indian passport. Since then I have great problems to get visas when

I travel around, but I'm not English nor Hindu. I'm a human being.

Ruben : You are a very special human being. You are easy to love.

Krishnamurti : I admit I'm different, but the transformation that has occurred in me can occur in any other human being. And nobody needs Krishnamurti or Dr. Ruben for that radical transformation, which is so necessary, to occur.

Ruben : Maybe not, but a serious dialogue helps.

Krishnamurti : With no guru. Dialogue without gurus.

Ruben : Could we say that you are being my guru without us wanting it and that I'm being your guru without it being my purpose?

Krishnamurti : Then there is a serious dialogue. You and I are seeing together the same thing at the same time. The most repugnant thing is to prostrate yourself before another human being and adore him or her.

(LONG PAUSE) (In vibrant silence)

Ruben : Someone told me you sometimes even faint out of sheer physical pain... What is that?

Krishnamurti : I call it "the process" but I don't understand it nor want to. I leave all the explanations about "the process", healing, and clairvoyance to doctors like yourself (laughing).

Ruben : I'd like you to tell me how to heal. I mean healing in its pristine and complete sense.

Krishnamurti : Again Dr. speaking (long pause) I prepared tea for you the other day. You found it bitter and left it. I had to ask you to finish it. You still have predilections, Dr. Gonzalez.

Ruben : So, to heal (with capital letters) you need to have no predilections.

Krishnamurti : No, no. It's necessary not to have predilections. Period. If you're content for something you're not content.

(LONG PAUSE)

Ruben : Would you summarize the teaching in only one sentence?

Krishnamurti : Attempt without effort to live with death in futureless silence.

Ruben : It sounds absurd.

Krishnamurti : Some time ago, in 1972, I spent a full morning with That without leaving my bed. I was completely quiet, before doing my Hatha yoga (only physical yoga, just to keep a flexible body)... that was like a flame in the centre of immensity. And the centre of immensity was my brain. Do you understand?

Ruben : Yes.

(LONG PAUSE)

Krishnamurti : Then, what are you waiting for?

Ruben : What? Are you by any chance saying that That is ready for me right now?

Krishnamurti : That's right. But you are too sad. What a waste! Then, what are you waiting for?

Ruben : I want to understand that sentence: "Die in silence without future". I think it would be better to say "attempt without effort to live in peace in futureless silence".

Krishnamurti : No. Death is the end of all you are afraid to lose: your attachments, your memory, your disappeared friends, your prestige as a children's surgeon. All that is the content of your consciousness. Can you get rid of it right now, now that you're young and healthy and not wait for 50 years for it to crumble by itself? It's easy for me to die.

Ruben : Saint Paul said: "I die every day".

Krishnamurti : Paul said "I die every day" and Dr. Gonzalez repeats what Paul says and nothing at all happens.

Ruben : You're more of a surgeon than I am.

Krishnamurti : Dr. Gonzalez, your brain has been as it is for the last million years. For how long will it be like that? Will you go to bed tonight with that brain of yours as it always has been? Habit, sorrow, anger, etc.?

Ruben : I wouldn't be here if I wanted to go to bed with this brain as it is. Nevertheless, I know I shouldn't accept what you say just blindly. I have to experience it. Would you be able to facilitate the experience of that which may transform my brain and my life?

Krishnamurti : If I was so stupid as to facilitate it, then all I say would become a theory or a technique, like so many others. You have to do it yourself, Dr. Gonzalez. Climb to the summit and look, or do you prefer to go to bed and beg me to describe it to you? Would you be satisfied with my description? Then you have no substance, then you are a second-hand human being. (PAUSE)

Ruben : How does mediocrity end?

Krishnamurti : As you get rid of the contents of human consciousness, will you get rid of all words?

Ruben : Without saying "Krishnamurti is talking to me".

Krishnamurti : Or he who listens is a "respectable Dr." You simply listen totally in pure silence.

Ruben : Nevertheless, even with no words, I'll be able to talk meaningfully from deep silence.

Krishnamurti : For the first time, quite sir. The word God is not God.

Ruben : Will it help to stop sex with my wife? (*)

Krishnamurti : Dr. Gonzalez, if you love, you love your wife, then you do what you will and there is beauty in what you do. Don't worry about sex, do it or don't. Now, let's be silent for a while because Mr. and Mrs. Lillifelt will be here soon. We will have to talk, because you know well Dr. Gonzalez, that I will not live forever. Perhaps ten years more and the chap will be gone.

{(*) The relationship with his wife ended three years later when she left their house, which he immediately got rid of. "Ever since then I live in the desert without securing my future."}

Krishnmurti died almost exactly ten years later.

Brockwood Park ; June 1978

In April 1976 Dr. Feldman-Gonzalez met Krishnamurti and Mrs. Zimbalist at an international meeting he attended with psychiatrists at the Carnegie Institute of Endowment in New York. It had been organized by Dr. David Shainberg from New York. The meetings were tape recorded, so he does not discuss them. When the last meeting ended he approached Krishnamurti as usual to shake his hand and make a few comments. This time Krishnamurti looked tired and only said a few words: "Did anybody listen?"

Krishnamurti used to make intentional pauses between words. "Please see Dr. Bohm in England and then see me in Brockwood, as soon as you can". The doctor just said goodbye. Krishnamurti was sweating and there was no joy on his face. It wasn't until June 18, 1978 that the doctor landed at Heathrow Airport in London (from Miami). He took a bus to Woking and from there a train to Petersfield. Mrs. Zimbalist was waiting for him at the station in Petersfield. He was dressed as informally as he could, and asked her why she was driving a Mercedes. She said it was a good car. He had the belief then that the teacher of the world should dress informally and even poorly and perhaps live uncomfortably.

Looking backwards he says he later tried to understand his lack of sensitivity and can only partially justify it, telling himself he was so eager to see the truth in Krishnamurti that he was doing at the same time everything possible to find out what he was hiding: either some esoteric teaching for the chosen few or some ugly business for some corporation.

But there was nothing of one nor of the other, he comments. "Krishnamurti was talking about the only thing that matters, and he was order, beauty, love and truth. Only it was too hard to believe!"

He shared meals with Krishnamurti for ten days in a row. He sat with him, Dr. Bohm and his wife, Mrs. Zimbalist, Mrs. Simmons and Mr. Narayan who was at that time Principal of the Rishi Valley School in India. On June 22 and 23 three cameras were set up to film the dialogues between Krishnamurti, Bohm, Narayan and Dr. Rahula, a Buddhist from Sri Lanka. Krishnamurti invited Dr. Feldman-Gonzalez to participate, and he, as usual, refused. During lunch, the following day he asked Krishnamurti what did he think of the Buddhist specialist.

Krishnamurti said, "You know there are many library mouses who can only repeat what they read, they are unable to live what they read. During the whole conversation there was not one moment of insight. He did nothing but compare the new (what Krishnamurti says) with the old (Buddhism). He compares everything with Buddha, he doesn't want to be a Buddha."

During one of those meals Narayan asked Krishnamurti to talk about reincarnation. Krishnamurti only said this: "What is it that continues?"

After lunch the doctor approached Krishnamurti who was walking alone with his dog Whisper under the trees. He told Krishnamurti he had been watching his sexual desire very closely the night before. He had been given a room where he slept by himself.

He asked, "Is there anything one can do not to repress the desire and not to free it in conduct?"

Krishnamurti said, "Be a light to yourself."

Talking to Whisper (the dog) he said: "Let's go Che-che".

By that time one of the male students (all between 14 and-22 years-old) had gone to the room of one of the girls. There was an ongoing administrative process to expel them both from the school. Krishnamurti decided he would discuss sex with the students but he didn't want the visiting parents who were staying in Brockwood that summer to participate.

The doctor started to leave but Krishnamurti called him: "You have to be present", he said. The students were angry during that meeting. One of them said to Krishnamurti, "You speak of freedom so much, why do you restrict sexual freedom in the school?"

Krishnamurti answered: "This school is like a home for you. Why wouldn't you take care of the school as you would take care of your home? You know we are under the laws of England and that we have to respect the laws; otherwise, they are going to close the school."

Dr. Feldman-Gonzalez met Krishnamurti soon after a series of long conversations with David Bohm regarding his concept of Holokinesis or holomovement.

Krishnamurti : Did you talk to Bohm?

Ruben : Yes. The place was small but the conversation was big. Dr. Bohm was patient enough to listen to all I had to say. He said my approach to perception could be very helpful for those who have the mind to listen. I'm trying to polish the language as much as I can.

Krishnamurti : That's good, but words have to be simple. Sometimes I have felt like creating a new language. But one has to speak to those who listen, and one has to use the words we have.

Ruben : Dr. Bohm agreed with me that whoever listens in unitary perception (holokinetic listening if you want) will have a changed molecular structure of the brain, of each neuron.

Krishnamurti : Quite, quite.

Ruben : That brain will make contact in a conscious way with what you call "the ground".

Krishnamurti : Perhaps, yes.

There was an art show later. The doctor discussed "Discipline" in Brockwood Park with Mathew Lazarus. When he met Krishnamurti, he told him:

Ruben : I was talking about "discipline" with one of the students. He said that western students define discipline in Brockwood as "strict". Eastern students consider it "loose".

Krishnamurti : Discipline is not a skill to learn. You either have it or you don't.

Ruben : Krishnaji, as I told you three years ago I don't see much meaning in working as a physician in a society that is getting more and more corrupt by the minute. You told me in 1975 that I shouldn't quit psychiatry (as I quit pediatric surgery) and that I should change psychiatry. What I see is that it is difficult for people to understand the basics of the new psychology and the new physics and even if they do understand nothing seems to happen... society continues to be based upon war...

Krishnamurti : Why do you separate God and work? Why can't you be joyful, peaceful, honest and creative in your work?

Around March 30, 1980; Ojai, California.

Ruben : Last year we couldn't talk too much. Mary (Zimbalist) takes good care of you. She didn't let me see you. Simple as that (laughing).

Krishnamurti : I asked her to live longer than I will, so she helps me to take care of "the horse". They claim that I take care of my body as a cavalry officer takes care of his horse. Maria is a good officer.

Ruben : I guess that without her it would be difficult to be even one minute by yourself, with so many people wanting to talk to you. People love you.

Krishnamurti : No, very few want to discuss anything serious. They fall in love with me and want to be close, that's all. It's not that they love.

Ruben : I'm glad to know Dr. David Bohm will talk with you and that the talks will be recorded. Please tell him I'd like to see him again.

Krishnamurti : Yes, we will record our talks with Dr. Bohm. I didn't know what we would do in the two days in California this time, but seems it will happen.

Ruben : I hope you talk about the problem of time. It was when I had my first contact with That, at the Frankfurt Airport in 1978, that I understood what is irrelevant time. It was the last thing I understood, the difference between relevant and irrelevant time. I think if somebody understands that difference right away That has to barge in.

Krishnamurti : Quite, Dr. Gonzalez.

Ruben : It's a pity that that "contact" is not a voluntary thing, because I would not like to live in any other way anymore. It's like healing or group-mind. It happens without one knowing how or why: It's perhaps semi-deliberate...

Krishnamurti : Don't get trapped in it when it happens.

Ruben : No, but it's fascinating.

Krishnamurti : It would be good to have you in our dialogue with Dr. Bohm, somebody who knows about the brain and intellectual psychology.

Ruben : Excuse me, but I'm not ready to participate in that dialogue. I'm going through a family crisis, my sons are in Argentina, and it's better not to talk about that. You might remember that last year, after having a walk with them, you told me: "Don't ask them what happened". That was in April 1979. Their mother left our house abruptly in August 1979. Is all this irrelevant time?

Krishnamurti : Yes, but you said you have tied the Ocean water. Don't avoid exposure Dr. Gonzalez. You already have something to say. I hope you'll participate and contribute.

Ruben : I'm very sorry I can't do it right now. It's not that I don't want it or that I'm afraid. I simply can't. I think I'm going through a small night of the soul, as they used to say.

Krishnamurti : I hope you can. Speak and expect no-thing. Don't expect to preserve your respectable merits, untie the ocean. The Ocean will flood Dr. Gonzalez. There will be nothing left of him.

(PAUSE)

Ruben : I'm thinking of working only four hours a day and living in the desert or by the sea, far from big cities. I made contacts in San Luis Obispo, Santa Barbara (with Dr. Ben whom you know so well), Ventura, Hawaii, etc. I want to live simply and with austerity. In November 1979 I refused an offer by Dr. Karl Pribram at Stanford University in California, to work with him in brain research.

Krishnamurti : You love and you do what you will. But austerity may not be simple.

Ruben : I got rid of everything I had.

Krishnamurti : Be careful that austerity be simple.

Ruben : What do you mean?

Krishnamurti : You may live in a mansion and spend the night in a grand hotel, as long as your future is not in your memory. He who dies rich has lived in vain.

Ruben : I agree. The doubts I have refer to the security of my two sons. I only don't want to have more children. I'm a pediatric surgeon and a pediatric neurologist—psychiatrist, but I don't know what to tell my children. The world is not fit for children.

Krishnamurti : Be responsible with the commitments you have taken upon yourself, but don't worry.

Ruben : I think my first commitment is to share the treasure of That when one truly lives in it. I'm spending everything I can spare traveling around the world and talking from That. That has come several times.

Krishnamurti : Yes, you look different. Since you come from Latin America, why not concentrate on Latin America? Tickets and hotels are more and more expensive every day and you know how difficult it is to get a visa sometimes. Nobody will pay your expenses from Latin America. Those who could pay will not listen and those who listen will not pay. Besides that, you need to take care of your health, you need exercise, Dr. Gonzalez. It's a problem to be in a hospital, all plans altered. That's what happened to me in 1977 when they operated upon my prostate. It was a chance to die and never come back, but there is a lot to do yet. You think it's generous to forget one's health, right?

Ruben : (laughing) I think it's the problem of almost

every physician, the idea that you have to take care of people's health and forget oneself. I was lucky to be born in a vegetarian home, that I never drank (alcohol) or used drugs or tobacco.

Krishnamurti : Beware of your generosity, Dr. Gonzalez, the end of the body shouldn't be precipitated by suicide nor the generosity of forgetting one's own body. What do you do when you talk with people in Latin America? Have you ever tried to ask a question in a group for nobody to answer? See what happens.

Ruben : I speak in Universities with professors and students. When riots and strikes start (which happens quite often due to the situation of oppression and plunder of which Latin America is victim) then I rent a hotel lecture-room, place an ad in a local paper (all quite expensive) and I invite the whole town, as I have done repeatedly in Caracas, Santiago, Buenos Aires, Rosario, several towns in Mexico and Lima. In Costa Rica there were no problems at the University (San Jose). Perhaps that's because Costa Rica has no Army. I speak of time and its relationship to consciousness, to perception. I speak of "Unitary Perception". Local gurus don't like me to talk because that's the end of their spiritual business. I also understand that when you told me "you talk". It's implicit. I'm the only one responsible for what I say. I do not represent you nor interpret your teaching.

Krishnamurti : Quite. Don't forget that in silence flowers an intuitive understanding. Do you talk of living an orderly life, peacefully and honestly?

That's not so difficult and that's the beginning. It's important to emphasize a radical change in daily life. Partial reforms (political, economic, ideological) are not enough.

Ruben : But they are urgently needed in Latin America, otherwise a lot of blood will be spilled.

Krishnamurti : yes, but without a radical psychological transformation a partial reform will only procrastinate the blood spill.

(PAUSE)

Ruben : If wars don't stop today, there will be war tomorrow.

(PAUSE)

Krishnamurti : Have you been flattered or invalidated?

Ruben : More flattered than invalidated. Both may be the same.

Krishnamurti : They are both rubbish, don't you see? They have done it with me, all my life. To adore or to mock is easier than listening. You know.

Ruben : I see it clearly. But change seems to be difficult.

Krishnamurti : Do you know that you can help those students to change?

Ruben : I hope so... but... that contradicts...

Krishnamurti : Give them all your compassion and all your intelligence and even the last minute of your time and energy, but learn to rest in silence. You work too much. Listen well to each one of them. In intelligence and compassion you are a little sun. You'll give light and warmth... and some will praise you, or will mock you from the shadows. Some others will sit in the sun.

(LONG PAUSE)

Ruben : Do you think I should speak without using my name (anonymously)?

Krishnamurti : Dr. Gonzalez you have four names, don't confuse me even more with your anonymity. Do not avoid exposure. Don't be afraid of losing anything. There's nothing to lose. You told me you're responsible for what you say, anonymous or not!

Ruben : What do I do with healing?

Krishnamurti : Healing the body is of secondary importance. Do what you will. But don't do it because someone wants it.

Ruben : What do you do with the aura?

Krishnamurti : Nothing. We have discussed this matter the first time we met. If you get trapped in something marvelous you'll not allow for the next marvelous thing to happen. Leave the aura alone. Leave kundalini alone. "That" cleanses everything. You don't need to worry.

Ruben : Sometimes you see something unbearable in someone you love. What do you do?

Krishnamurti : Do you have predilections? Or will you look for some reason for it? It seems unbearable to love someone who will not get interested in That. There is a brother I would like to get interested... he resists... but that's that.

Ruben : The saddest thing for me is to see what human beings could be but are not. I would even stop watching the news, but it's hard.

(LONG PAUSE)

Krishnamurti : I watch the news sometimes, or else someone else summarizes them for me. The spiritual state of mankind is deplorable. Don't you see how urgently necessary your own transformation is, Dr. Gonzalez? Every child should travel around the world. Then they could cry for all mankind and they would stop thinking as Argentineans, Hindus, Russians, American, Japanese, etc.

Ruben : Nothing seems to be enough to understand something so simple.

Krishnamurti : Your own total psychological transformation is enough. It's enough to get rid of mankind's consciousness. It's necessary to do so and that is the pure silence and the pure peace of the brain. But that can't be left for tomorrow, if one is serious.

Ruben : Silence without name.

Krishnamurti : It's like a house which doesn't have a place for silence... it will be a house with a lot of activity, plenty of noise, but there That will not enter. There has to be a room in each house where the only thing you can do there is to be silent and nothing else. That room will be the flame of the house.

Ruben : Then each home would be like a temple...

Krishnamurti : Each home would be a home without sorrow, that is a good home.

(LONG PAUSE)

Krishnamurti : Well Dr. Gonzalez, it's time to go now. I'm sorry.

Ruben : Krishnaji, before we go... I hope you give me the names of those you think have understood you best, even when not absolutely well. I'd like to talk with all of them.

Krishnamurti : They are few, so find them and meet them. Untie the ocean together.

Ruben : Thank you for all, my friend.

Five years in Ojai

Dr. Feldman-Gonzalez saw Krishnamurti many times in the last five years of his life. He says he can't remember the dates well except that his meetings with him happened during the two or three weeks the public talks in Ojai were being held. It was clear to him that he was not going to depend on Krishnamurti to anything, but he still was intent on discovering "the complete silence of the mind". Whenever they met in Ojai it was with David Bohm and a small group of friends, or occasionally by chance close to Arya Vihar (his residence) or at the Oak Grove School. One day he told K the eternal That, the immense joyful energy... had "touched" him. He also told him that very soon it left him. The meaning of That touching him was immense, it made him very strong during the few big adversities of his life.

He asked K, "Why doesn't That come more often?"

Krishnamurti said, "What do you do with your energy?"

Around 1981 a birthday party was organized for K (in May) by the people working at the four Foundations. Krishnamurti arrived and stood in silence for three or four minutes. Suddenly a gentleman with a Bostonian or perhaps English accent approached Krishnamurti and said: "I understand you are a Brahmin from India".

Krishnamurti said, "I only have a passport from India".

He soon left the party.

May 1983; Krishnamurti had public talks in Ojai rather late in the Spring of 1983. Dr. Feldman-Gonzalez was with his two sons: Sebastian age nine and Demian age eight. They couldn't get a motel in Ojai. They were all full. They spent the nights at the Holiday Inn in Ventura right beside the Pacific Ocean. The sons were happy. They had the sea, and Ojai was only thirty minutes away by car.

It is claimed that "Ojai" means "The Nest of God" in the local American-Indian tongue. On the morning of Saturday, May 14th, 1983 they arrived at the Oak Grove School in Ojai (Founded by Krishnamurti in 1974) at about 9.30 A.M. They parked the car and went for a slow walk under a sunny light-blue sky among the oak trees. There was a delightful breeze between the blue mountains and the ocean. There were already more than 1000 people for the lecture that would start two hours later. The doctor met many friends from different parts of the world.They were elated by their mutual company and by the expectation of listening to Krishnamurti in person again. The blend of nature, friendship and the sacred is beauty itself. And that day they were deep into the glorious light of beauty and the rare presence of love.

Krishnamurti talked for an hour or so about the deplorable spiritual state of mankind. Three thousand people listened in silence. It was only Krishnamurti's voice and the breeze among the Oak trees. Hundreds of birds were chirping. He said we have to be a light to ourselves because "there is no one to go to". Social and individual corruption grows. He said it's perfectly possible to relate without a shadow of conflict. At the end he shook hands with Dr. Feldman-Gonzalez and his two sons. "It's good to see you for a moment", he said.

Demian said, "Krishnamurti has cold hands, Dad".

Dr. Feldman-Gonzalez said, "Krishnamurti is eighty-eight years old, and he was talking for more than an hour under the trees in the breeze".

It was during that weekend that they met at Arya Vihara in Ojai. There was a circle of chairs with at least ten people sitting with Krishnamurti. It was three or four PM, and it was easy to lose track of time in that kind of atmosphere after a cup of tea. After Krishnamurti joined them they remained in silence. One had to absorb his presence before any action was possible. At one point he asked, "Am I a freak?"

Ruben : "You may not be a freak but possibly the genetic pool you come from makes you definitely more able to be free from the influence of human memory (both individual and philogenetic). That has made you more able to be in total contact with reality, while we are at best only partially in contact with it."

Krishnamurti said something close to the following, "We may have genetic differences but we are all able to 'touch' the ground or the totality of the mind, and that ground is the most important thing for human life".

Ruben : "The ground being the cosmic mind or the holokinetic source of life...."

Krishnamurti said, "The ground being complete silence of the mind (he emphasized the word 'complete'), then we can talk".

He finished.

Ruben : "Is there something external that comes to us (or to Krishnamurti) in certain specific circumstances?

Krishnamurti said, "It may come now when two or more meet to discuss seriously, which means with no wish for money or success and letting all the masks that protect us drop off. Water will not know what water is. We can only discuss what water is not. You may explain water well but you have to swim in the sea as well".

Ruben : "We are in California. If you had to only use the words from the Bible how would you tell me what you just said to me?"

Krishnamurti said: "It's revelation. Something that happens every time I speak. But now, since that happens, I prefer to use my own words which are less loaded with distortions".

Ruben: "Tell us more about That."

Krishnamurti said, "It's too big for words".

A long silence followed. The doctor finally asked, "what will we do, the ones that have tasted a few drops of that water?"

Krishnamurti said, "Those few will have to shout from the housetops before it's too late for mankind".

The doctor told him that some people were angry at him for the way he had said some things. Many seemed unable to forgive Krishnamurti for what he had said in Saanen in 1980: "God is disorder and if man is God's creation, God has to be horrible, a monstrous entity. God must be disorder since we live in disorder. If he made us like He is and we are killing each other, then He must be monstrous".

Krishnamurti said: "What God are we talking about? Is it the God that man made? Those that get angry want to substitute the experience of God, the man-made God. It's not so easy. That word is disorder, not the experience. Where the word is, experience is not. Where experience is, there may or may not be the word".

When the last talk of 1985 ended in Ojai in May Dr. Feldman-Gonzalez decided he wouldn't attend any more Krishnamurti talks. Krishnamurti died in February 1986 anyway. It struck him, after his death, while he was listening to the last of his talks in England, held in 1985, that he said: "I will not use the word meditation anymore". He had asked him to do that several times. One day they were at an orange grove in Arya Vihar, simply enjoying the scent of spring in silence.

The doctor said, "I worry the schools are going to become elitist and that only the wealthy will be able to send their children to them." Krishnamurti said: "We have to work with what we have and we have to talk with the words we have. I was born in a very poor home and some of my brothers died from tuberculosis or malnutrition. But look at me! I'm doing very well, huh?"

The doctor said, "you were lucky you had teachers like Leadbeater who was even clairvoyant."

Krishnamurti said, "Yes, I was very lucky. Leadbeater was temporarily clairvoyant, and I was lucky that everything he said entered through my right ear and left through the left."

They were sitting with David Bohm and Krishnamurti. Dr. Feldman-Gonzalez told Krishnamurti: "From the conversations the three of us have had, including the one with Dr. Sheldrake, one may infer that when one human mind is consummate in intelligence and love, that mind will inexorably influence (non-verbally) in an energetic (holokinetic) way, all human minds at the same time. Now if Krishnamurti is totally transformed or consummate, how come one doesn't see it more in people around us or even in the whole world? How come the sorrow, the brutality, the vulgarity, the insensitivity of people is not reduced? Why don't we see the transformation more?

At that point Krishnamurti told Dr. Bohm, "Professor Bohm, you have been a co-worker of Albert Einstein but even so one can still talk to you without a mask. (Krishnamurti smiled)... how would you answer that question? Why don't we see the change?"

Dr. Bohm meditated for a few seconds and said: "As a physicist I only know that 99% of all phenomena occurring in matter and energy are invisible."

Recollections and Assessments

Krishnamurti has been variously assessed, the assessments reflecting different points of view from where he is assessed. Krishnamurti has been usually critical of any tradition as a handmaiden of thought rather than insight.

David Frawley, writing on Krishnamurti and the question of tradition has this to offer: In California he happened to end up for a few years at Ojai, the town where Krishnamurti gave his yearly talks, which he attended regularly. He became familiar with the Krishnamurti community and made friends with several older members of the group, most who were ex-Theosophists.

Krishnamurti's thoughts had a logic that appealed to Frawley's revolutionary and anti-authority mentality. He was a kind of spiritual anarchist. Though he was in favour of meditation and the spiritual life, he was against gurus and structured practices. Yet given Frawley's connections with the Vedas and Vedanta he couldn't accept his wholesale rejection of tradition and technique, or his criticism of mantra.

"Krishnamurti was, on one hand, a typically self-alienated Indian intellectual criticizing his own culture. But, on the other hand, he possessed a genuine meditative mind in harmony with the same tradition, a strange contradiction but one that was appealing to people who could not relate to traditions. He had important teachings on perception and on the workings of the mind and emotions that added much depth to my meditation.

Krishnamurti wanted to create a teaching that was

universal, that was not culturally limited or conditioned, and did not require any identity in order to follow. While this was a noble endeavor it failed to note the organic nature of life.

In refusing to align with any tradition his teaching became limited to perhaps the most limited factor. It became a one man teaching or one-man tradition — a Krishnamurti teaching. All tradition is not bad. Otherwise we should leave our infants in the woods and let them raise themselves without authority, tradition or interference. We all follow various traditions in life. We are part of a society and a collective evolution."

"We as individuals don't invent our own language, much less our own spiritual teachings," Frawley goes on . "We have to take the good that the collective culture gives us and carry it further along. An authoritarian tradition that does not allow open questioning but projects a dogma as truth is certainly harmful. But a cultural tradition that promotes spirituality and creativity is very helpful. For example, a musical tradition provides the instruments and tools for musicians to grow. Spiritual traditions can be helpful springboards for self-realization. The problem arises when their tools are applied mechanically, which is unfortunately too often the case."

"Real knowledge has a tradition and an authority," Frawley claims, "just as there is in science, but it is a matter of direct experience, not of mere belief. This is the basis of the real Vedic tradition. One important thing I did learn from Krishnamurti was not to blindly follow anyone who called himself a guru. Later I learned that it is particularly dangerous to follow a guru who does not represent or have the sanction of any real tradition. The Vedic view allows thinking and debate and can even accept a Krishnamurti who rejects the tradition for his insights on meditation."

Dr. S. Balasundaram was a former Secretary of the Krishnamurti Foundation India. In a talk at the Adyar

Convention 1995, J. Krishnamurti Birth Centenary Year, he narrated a story to illustrate his association with Krishnamurti. (Published in 'Krishnamurti As I Knew Him, pp.126-131, The Theosophist, December 1996, Vol.118, No. 3. Reproduced by permission of The Theosophical Publishing House, Adyar, Chennai 600 020.)

"A rich brahmin, unaware of life's impermanence, had built himself a large house. The Buddha sent Ananda to this old man to find out why he has done this and teach him the four noble truths. Instead of listening to Buddha's teachings the brahmin just went on about the purpose of each of the many rooms in his house. As soon as Ananda left, the old man fell ill and died. And Buddha said that the brahmin was like a spoon that tastes not the flavour of the soup."

Neither Dr. Balasundaram nor any of his relatives were Theosophists. But his wife Vina Visalakshi used to live in Madras and had many friends in the TS. She knew Krishnaji, so he also came to know him. Dr. Balsundaram was a research scholar in the Indian Institute of Science and by nature a sceptic. He never sought out or met anyone. But somehow he met Krishnaji in 1947 along with his wife. From the first day onwards K said to him a number of times, "Balasundaram, I am your friend." In work, in all kinds of situations, he was a friend, which came through in his presence and tremendous affection. When he came to India after the war, he was very affectionate and wanted to meet young people and get to know them. There used to be a pandal (awning) outside the house in Stirling Road, Madras, where he stayed and he used to sit there most of the time.

One day Dr. Balasundaram saw a gentleman in dhoti and kurta, with a purple cap and a bundle of detective stories under his arm, walking into his room. He looked and thought. 'This cannot be a holy man.' After some time this man came out and went away. As his curiosity got the better of him, he went quickly inside and saw the bundle next to Krishnamurti. He asked: "Sir, do you read these things?' He said: 'Yes, I do. But I am a slow reader." Then I asked: "Who was it who brought these books to you?" He said: "Don't you know him? That was Jinarajadasa, the President of the Theosophical Society." This was in 1947.

In 1948, Dr. Balasundaram was in Bangalore at the Institute of Science. Krishnamurti did not go back that summer to Europe or America, but stayed in Ooty and went from there to Bangalore. They were looking after him, being with him most of the time. Then they asked Mr. Maurice Frydman, who had known Krishnamurti from his Ommen days, to stay with him in Vikram Sarabhai's house.

Dr. Balasundaram used to see Krishnamurti every day. After the second or third day K said to him, "Mr Balasundaram, I cannot walk with these chappals (sandals). Can you get me some Pathan chappals (the strapped ones like Roman sandals)?" So he got a Chinese cobbler to make them. The next morning, Dr. Balasundaram walked to his place before breakfast and found him sitting in a corner, polishing the new sandals. He stood behind him in awe and said, "Sir, I can do this for you, please." He turned around, still polishing the sandals and said: 'You know who taught me to polish shoes? The shoeblack of King Edward the Seventh." Dr. Balasundaram comments: "It was actually so; he was not telling me a story. This indicates the care and the regal way the TS had looked after him and brought him up. He never talked about the past, but suddenly something would flash up from the past in his consciousness."

One day, Maurice Frydman and his friend Wanda Dynowska, who used to call herself Uma Devi and stayed in the TS at Sevashrama, came to see him. She had translated many theosophical works and also Krishnamurti's books and sent them through underground channels to Poland in the days when Communism was supreme. It was a tremendous work. Uma Devi's brother was killed during the War and in 1948 news was still trickling in and she had just heard that somebody else had died, which made her very unhappy. So

Frydman, who always used to make things a little philosophical, said: 'What should one's attitude be to the dead?'

Krishnamurti answered: "The Bible has it, Sir: Let the dead bury the dead." That was all; nothing else.

Some days before Krishnamurti left after a stay of six weeks, Frydman said: "This chap Balasundaram should be put to work. He is very capable, but I cannot get him to work. Krishnaji, you are the only person who can persuade him. So, you should tell him to work with me, and we will start." Dr. Balasundaram knew Frydman had his own way of doing things. In 1950, for one year he was the Secretary of the Krishnamurti Foundation and also of its Rajghat Center. He turned it upside down, says Dr. Balasundaram. So, when Frydman said that he should work with him, Dr. Balasundaram replied: "I will never work with Maurice Frydman. He says one thing and does another. He is most unreliable." Krishnaji just looked at him and responded: "How can you say such a thing? He may have changed even at the last minute. What you say may be true, but he may have changed." You see, Dr. Balasundaram comments, this was so obvious. "The teacher was thus teaching. His teaching flashed through even small things. In this case the lesson was that I should live without an image. It was a shocking lesson."

Krishnaji remarked: "I am just poking you to live, to become alive." Dr. Balasundaram's wife was a musician and, as many people knew, she was going deaf in one ear. Towards the end of his stay, Krishnaji said: "I am going away in a week. If you want me to help your wife I will see what I can do for her." He did not know what K meant. Then K added: "Amma (he always called Annie Besant Amma or mother) always got up at four o'clock in the morning, made herself a strong brew of coffee, and then started her work. Often she had a nagging headache." So one day she said: "Son, put your hand on my head; that might help." "I just put my hand on her head like this and her headache subsided. Then I realized that there was something in my hands. It sometimes works and sometimes does not. If you wish I will try it on Visalakshi." He did, and it did not work.

Suddenly Dr. Balasundaram decided to retire from the Indian Institute of Science and go to America to make some money and then completely retire. But one day he received a telegram from Rishi Valley, 'Krishnaji wants to see you urgently.' He drove down in his old car thinking he would be back for work the next morning or evening, but he stayed for three days. Krishnamurti said: "Are you going to America for research?" When he replied he would return in about three years, he said: "Why don't you retire now and help these people?" That is how he went to Rishi Valley, and without having taught in any school or college became the principal of the School. "Things always happened around him and there were always changes. The three-day session I had with Krishnaji jolted me completely out of the image I had of a religious man. Krishnaji lived in the world and took part in its life as you would have read in his Commentaries, but he was not of the world. He was totally out of it."

Dr. Balasundaram recalls that Krishnamurti could not bear the sun, for he had had sunstroke. He never went out for a walk before almost sundown. So Dr. Balasundaram used to do a lot of driving with him during which they had a great many conversations. Sometimes they were trivial. At other times K was tremendously interested. For instance, in ancient history, in the sky, in astronomy, in the stars, and all kinds of things, and he would talk and say, "Look at the Southern Cross". Sometimes there would be more people in the car, sometimes only the two of them. Dick Balfour Clarke would sometimes come cycling down from the TS to see him off.

Krishnamurti was very well-informed, Dr. Balasundaram recalls, but he read very little and also slowly. "I have never seen him read any religious books. Becoming very serious once when Life magazine produced a statistical table after the 1968 Olympics showing India at the bottom of the scale, he said: "Has it occurred to you why this country has not produced one outstandingly creative individual in so many years in science, art, music, and so forth, and this for a country which has all these beautiful sculptures and temples? Why did it not produce a single truly creative individual lately who is internationally known?" He went on badgering him. He used to address Dr. Balasundaram as 'Old boy', or 'Balasundaram', or 'Sir', it meant you were in for the cudgel. He continued "Have you not thought about it? How can you educate people if you are not aware of this?" Then Dr. Balasundaram threw the question back: "What would you say?" He replied that it was an old trick to throw the question back, but added: "I'll tell you, watch. Whenever there has been a great efflorescence of art, music, poetry, and so forth, it appears after a great religious period. What do we see after the Buddha appeared? The Ajanta and Ellora caves! If anyone creates nowadays something like that he would be acclaimed worldwide. Anonymous people did that!" He went on viewing the whole world and then said: "True religious feeling is the mother of all creativity. This country has let it go." He was very serious about it, Dr. Balasundaram comments.

He was affectionate, according to Dr. Balasundaram, but could also be explosive at times. It was so when he said: "You have to do something." Dr. Balasundaram replied: "What can one man do?" Then K turned round and said: "Do not ever say that again: What can one man do? Napoleon was one man. Hitler was one man, the Buddha was one man. So for good or evil things have been changed by one person. You have to go to the root. If you do not discover the root, you can do only something on the periphery. This goes for education and for everything."

Krishnaji had a great presence, Dr. Balasundaram testifies. "I do not remember ever sitting with legs crossed in his presence. It is not that one was not consciously respectful; I just could not do it. It is like Rom Landau says in his book *God is My Adventure,* when he went to see Krishnaji in 1934. At that time he used to smoke regularly, but he wrote: 'I forgot to pick up a cigarette in those fifteen days, because I forgot that I was a smoker.' Krishnaji had a tremendous presence that affected some people that way. Other people were not affected in the same way, one cannot say why. Often I have seen villagers and people who did not know him at all stand back and bow to greet him when he walked by."

Dr. Balasundaram comments that scriptures say that one of the major causes of man's illusion is dehātma-bhāva, believing that you are the body. But in Krishnamurti this was never there. He used to treat his body as a separate entity which he had to look after, clothe, bathe, feed with the right kind of food and so forth. Krishnaji used to treat it as though it was a precious instrument to look after.

There is much talk about what Krishnamurti meant by freedom, according to Dr. Balasundaram. He meant not doing whatever one likes to do or indulging oneself: but freedom from likes and dislikes. Once he told his nephew Narayan, "If I had not subjected this body to such an amount of travel, it would have lasted four hundred years." Dr. Balasundaram asked: "Did he say four hundred or a hundred?" Narayan repeated, 'four hundred". Dr. Parchure said to Krishnaji one day, "Your liver is not at all right. Take bitter gourd juice every morning at breakfast." And he did it without wincing—no likes or dislikes. He lived only for delivering his message.

When he was over eighty, a friend of Dr. Balasundaram in Orissa said: "There are so many places in India where he has not been, can you not persuade him to come here?"

Krishnamurti said: "How can I travel for two days to go to some place? And after that travel, what am I supposed to do?" As Dr. Balsundaram could be a little free with him, having known him long, he said: "You could give *darsan* there." He rejoined: "Talking is my mètier, and I will talk and talk until I drop down dead. Full stop!" And he did just that. He went through with his mission until physically he could not do it any more. That was the extraordinary zeal with which he lived.

When he came to Rishi Valley, or elsewhere, he would say, "I want to put hot coals underneath those people." Although he had tremendous love, he would badger people in order to awaken them. Robert Linsson, in his book *Living Zen,* compares some of Krishnamurti's teachings with those of Zen; he did not always treat people with kid gloves. Dr. Balasundaram said to him once, "Sir, you want constant revolution, like Mao in China. You are all the time changing things." He answered: "I want to create a crisis for you and for people. It is all in the programme, but you will not have it, neither will they." So his 'programme' was not only his teaching, but his approach which could be like a tornado at times. "I come like a storm," he said, "and when I go people are relieved."

When Dr. Balasundaram was still young as a Principal of Rishi Valley School, one day Krishnamurti arrived. After about two days he started to question him: "Balasundaram, have you produced one boy who is different, who is in an other-worldly direction? And is there one teacher who is?" He was very insistent. At first Dr. Balasundaram offered some explanation that things were better, but nothing like that would do for him. He was at him during breakfast, lunch and dinner. On the evening of the third day they went for a walk. After about one kilometer he asked. "Where is the new moon?" He seldom talked much or discussed serious matters during walks. We looked around, then suddenly he laughed and said, "Balasundaram, this is like my walk with George Arundale. He was my teacher, and at one time in Wimbledon we were not on speaking terms. This was around the years 1919 or 1918. We used to walk four miles a day without a word being spoken. It was just like this walk, because we have not spoken a word either." Dr.

Balasundaram did not think it was very funny and remained a little glum. Then he took both my hands and shook them while he questioned: "Old boy, are you hurt by what I have been saying these three days?" I said: "Maybe a little, Sir." He dug his hand into my chest and said: 'Old boy, remember, if you are hurt, something is wrong with you!' He repeated that sentence three times.

Krishnamurti was such a great teacher, in Dr. Balasundaram's view, that he taught not only through his talks, but through his discussions, and various other means. It was not only his words that affected people, but that something else which came through which entered one's blood like a vaccine. He had this extraordinary something which is not so apparent when studying his books. "Why I did not change while I kept on listening to him, I cannot say. It is a mystery. He himself said towards the end of his life: 'I have spoken for so many years and people are not transformed. There are only a couple of people who are a little different.' His only concern over the last forty years of his life was that people should change fundamentally."

They used to have performances, ballets and all that kind of thing in Rishi Valley, and many villagers would come. Every evening Dr. Balasundaram used to take K out to the huge banyan tree in the campus. One evening, just after the meal he stood up and holding on to the table said: "Balasundaram, they have started making tapes. Is it all going to stay in books and on tapes? Only that?" What could he answer? He was stunned. Then Krishnamurti went to wash, and when he came back, Dr. Balasundaram took him in total silence to the banyan tree.

After he passed away, in 1990, they sent Dr. Balasundaram to the International Trustees Conference in Brockwood which K had initiated in 1973. They put into the participants' hands eleven series of 'Discussions' held in 1977, and they were told that these were being given them to read and meditate on. Their gist was: "This man will be gone in ten years' time. What will you offer somebody who comes and asks about these teachings and about the man? Will you show him a videotape, or hand him a book? What will you Trustees show? Unless you yourself change, your witness unto truth is all in vain, as the Bible has it."

In 1995 Dr. Balasundaram went to America for the birth centenary, and met many people, among them Professor Allan Anderson. He was Professor Emeritus of Religion, Santiago University. He said he saw Krishnamurti only once during his dialogues in 1974. Then he remarked: "The person is no more, but his spirit abides.' Many had been really touched in some way by his message, including a man who had been a prisoner in jail. Maybe people were not transformed as Krishnaji expected, but a great many were touched and affected by his teachings, which was noticeable in the conduct of their personal affairs and professional dealings.

Here is a recollection of Prof. P. Krishna, Rector, Rajghat Education Centre, Krishnamurti Foundation India, Varanasi, India, based on an article titled 'Krishnamurti As I Knew Him' published in the May 1997 issue of *The Theosophist*, pp.321-327. Vol.118, No.8. (Reproduced by permission of The Theosophical Publishing House, Adyar, Chennai 600 020, India.)

A dialogue between Arjuna and Krishna in the Gita is apposite for describing Krishnamurti, according to Prof. Krishna. Arjuna asks Krishna about the liberated man. How does such a person live, how does he act, how does he eat and sleep? Krishna's reply in sum is: Outwardly, he is the same as everybody else, he eats and sleeps and lives like them. And yet he is totally different, because he does not do any of these things for the same reason as the ordinary man. There is a dimensional difference in his consciousness. And that is important, not his accomplishments, education, erudition, or all the lectures he may give and so on. Even without those things, his importance would be no less. How does one communicate that? One senses it in his presence, but it is not possible to put it in words. What one can put into words are only the outer actions, the words that one heard, the thoughts that one had, and so on, one cannot convey the state of mind or consciousness from which those words emanated. It is something that one senses between the lines.

Prof. Krishna did not know Krishnamurti well. He never worked closely with him or lived or travelled with him. He was only a rather active, ardent student of his teachings, who took every opportunity to have dialogues with him, to listen to his talks, and put questions as were in his mind.

His first encounter with his teachings was in 1955 when Krishna was seventeen. During a summer vacation, while going through one of his father's cupboards, he came across a small booklet, *Talks to Students.* He had not heard about Krishnamurti nor did he know anything about him. Because it was titled 'Talks to Students' he began reading it. It addressed all those questions which arose in his adolescent mind, and which his teachers never discussed. K was talking with students about whether respect is the same thing as fear: 'Why do you get up from your seat when the teacher enters the class?' He was asking girls "Why do you put the 'tika' (red dot) on your forehead?", not in a derogatory sense nor finding fault, but earnestly, "Do you know why you do all these things?' What is the significance? Have you ever questioned yourself? Why are you afraid of examinations? We do not talk about these things as part of education. So it fascinated Krishna greatly and he read more of his books.

Then Krishna went to his father to ask about Krishnamurti, and he told him the story of how he grew up in the Theosophical Society, how he was 'discovered', and so on. Krishna was quite taken with *The First and Last Freedom.* It created a certain image or picture in my mind of someone like a Buddhist saint, calm and imperturbable. So when

Krishna first met K he was taken aback and a bit shocked, because he was not at all like the image he had in his mind.

In the winter of 1958, K was staying in Delhi with Mr. Shiva Rao, a family friend. Krishna was studying for his Master's degree in Physics at Delhi University, and was keenly interested in meeting the author of the books he had read. So Mr. Shiva Rao invited him to lunch with him.

Before lunch, when he was introduced to Krishnamurti, he asked Krishna, "What are you doing?", and Krishna said, "I am learning physics at the University". And he said, "Why are you studying Physics?" Krishna found it a bit odd, because everyone studies at the university, and he said, "Well, in order to get a job, make a living, and settle down in life". And K called to Shiva Rao, "Look at this young boy, nineteen years of age, and he is already worried about settling down and getting married and making a living!" Krishna felt small, he felt K was finding fault with him. So he said, "What is wrong with doing that, Sir?", and he said, "Do anything you like: beg, borrow or steal, but don't worry about the future, about how you are going to make a living." Krishna was appalled! He asked, "Steal?", and K answered, "No, Sir, not steal. I mean do anything, but do it with passion, because you like to do it, not because you want to make a living". He added, 'This is the trouble with our education. The whole purpose of it is just to make a living and get a job. We have turned education into such a small, horrid affair!"

That was like him, not trying to please or impress people. He was spontaneous, with no pretense, and full of passion. Lunch with him used to go on along with conversation in between. Once Krishna asked him, "Sir, I have read that when you were in the Theosophical Society, people sat in a closed room and had sessions in order to talk with dead spirits, and these were occult phenomena. Was that all hallucination?' He replied, "No, those things exist, but it is another form of power. It has nothing to do with goodness. Therefore I am not interested in it." Then he added, 'Of course, the mind has infinite powers of hallucination". Later on Krishna wondered, what did he mean? And he felt he was trying to convey that occult phenomena, telepathy, ESP, and other powers, do exist, but if one is not interested in power—money, or muscle, or position or status—why would one want to cultivate occult power?'

He said his memories of early childhood were completely wiped out. Whatever experiences he had since 1922 had obliterated those memories from his brain. He said he did not remember Adyar, although he had lived there. He said, "I cannot recall my brother Nitya's face. I can barely recall Amma's face" (meaning Mrs. Besant). Then he added, mysteriously to Krishna, "Of course, I can recall it, Sir, if I want to." Krishna was never able to make head or tail of that.

Krishna used to put many questions to him at the end of his talks. Once after one of those question sessions he went to greet him (and K would hold Krishna's hands very affectionately) and he said: "Too many questions, my boy, too many questions". The love, the affection he felt in K's presence he found difficult to describe.

From 1959 onwards, after doing his Master's degree, Krishna was at Banaras Hindu University as a Research Scholar in Physics, and K came to Banaras and gave talks in Rajghat. Krishna would go on his bicycle about eight or ten miles from the city to attend his lectures whenever he could. In one of his lectures K said: "A disciplined mind is a lazy mind." To Krishna a disciplined person was active, regular, attending to all his work. So when he asked K what he meant, "If it is not lazy, why does it need to discipline itself? If you have to get up at six o'clock in the morning and if you are not lazy, you get up! Discipline is not required for that. But if you are lazy, you need a lot of discipline. So the man who is trying to discipline himself is lazy."

In those few words, Krishna coments, K explained the duality of the opposites. When a person tries to cultivate courage it means he is afraid. Trying to be nonviolent, implies one is violent. Whenever we try to pursue anything, its opposite is present. Instead of pursuing the opposite, one should concern oneself with ending laziness. Laziness has a cause, maybe the person does not eat or sleep or exercise properly, or his body is aching and he does not have adequate energy. Instead of correcting that, if one seeks to cultivate discipline, it amounts to perpetuating laziness, and a tussle goes on between the two.

When Krishnamurti talked to young students, he would talk to them at their simple level. With David Bohm, he would talk at the level of David Bohm. In every case, he was equally full of enthusiasm, irrespective of who he was talking to. He did not assess people in terms of position or achievements. Krishna claims he always found K alert, sensitive, watchful, aware. There was no trace of laziness in him. There was an overflowing affection for everybody, but that did not mean that he would compromise on truth or avoid it if bitter.

In the 1960s, after a talk when Krishna went and stood near him, a gentleman from the audience came, full of praise, saying, "Lovely talk, Sir, lovely talk; what a marvellous talk!" After he had gone Krishnaji looked at Krishna and said, "It is an insult." To Krishna that meant: Here K was at pains to expound the truths about life, and instead of exploring that, this person only says what a beautiful talk. He would take as an insult what others would normally take as a great compliment.

Krishna wanted to photograph him, and carried a camera the whole day. But in those days he would not allow any photographs to be taken. Nor would he allow any one to take notes of his lectures. He did not want his lectures to be reduced to a form of knowledge. He wanted them to be an experience of seeing together whatever he was talking about. So he would repeatedly stress that he was not giving a lecture: "This is not something that I am trying to pass on to you—some information that you don't have. We are looking at life, together like two friends." Although he was talking to the whole gathering, he would emphasize that it was essentially a one-to-one talk between two friends, and that we should use his statements like a mirror held before ourselves, to look at our own lives, and verify if what he was saying was true or not, not blindly accept it.

Naturally, he set no value on agreement or disagreement as such, because that has no meaning. He said, "I may agree with you or both of us may be agreeing on something or we may disagree, and still not know what is truth. Seeing truth has value—not agreeing or disagreeing, or carrying opinions for or against."

During a dialogue in Brockwood in 1977, with Prof. David Bohm, Asit Chandmal, and others, Krishna remembers starting it with a question which they had already discussed among ourselves: "Sir, you say that one is not able to see 'What is' clearly, in an undistorted way, because of the conditioning and colouration of the mind produced by the self. But because we are not able to see the truth, 'What is', because of this colouration, this self continues. When will this vicious circle end?" He went into it, and they talked about it. Every time they asked him a question, he looked at it afresh, without bringing definitions or conclusions from previous inquiries. There was a quality of enquiry, never holding on the past, because it is important to see the truth through cognition rather than as memory. So he went into Krishna's question, "I am not sure if the self must be completely absent for insight to occur, or if insight can be so great that it wipes away the self. This is not a process in which you first get rid of the colouration, and then you have the insight, or that insight comes first and then the ego is washed away. It is simultaneous."

When Krishna asked him, "Sir, were you once part of the field and did you step out of it or were you always out of the field?", he said: "I question it too." He also questioned why in the case of this little boy Krishnamurti, brought up in the Theosophical Society, who could not pass any examinations being rather dull by normal standards, his mind did not get conditioned like that of everybody else. Why is it that he kept that openness to perceive something new? When you pick up a young boy and bring him up to be the Dalai Lama, he becomes the Dalai Lama. So it would have been normal for him to have become a great Theosophist, the head of the Theosophical Society. How did he come upon something totally new? Why do all the other children get conditioned, and find it difficult to come out of that conditioning, whereas this child learned from every experience?

In 1925, when he was 30, while on a ship bound for India, he heard of his brother's death and was overcome by great sorrow. But when he landed in India he was completely peaceful, and from aboard the ship he wrote to Mrs. Besant, "What I experienced was not sorrow. I am now through with it. I have cheated death." It seems that he was saying that the death of his brother came in the form of personal sorrow: and that it could have trapped him into a state of self-pity, and so on, as it would have with most of us; instead he saw through the personal sorrow, understood the significance of death and attachment, and freed himself from it. What is the quality of a consciousness or mind which goes through experience and instead of collecting a complex, prejudice, or new conditioning, sees the truth and frees itself?

A man once told Krishnamurti that he was very lucky to have been brought up in the Theosophical Society with teachers like CWL and Mrs. Besant, and he said: "Yes, I was very fortunate to have teachers like them." Then the man said, "We are not so lucky, we are going through ordinary institutions. How can we come upon truth?" And he responded: "Sir, I was lucky because whatever they told me went into one ear and out of the other." He was not being disparaging. He only meant that they did not condition his mind into what they were teaching. His whole teaching is that one must come upon the truth by oneself, and not accept it from a teacher, because then it becomes just words, and is not 'seeing.'

The last time K visited India, in 1985, Krishna was having lunch with him at Rajghat and as often happened he asked questions that nobody ever asked: "Sir, has the brahmin disappeared from this country?" Krishna said: "It depends on what you mean by brahmin, Sir. One fourth of the population here think of themselves as brahmins." And he said, "No, not by birth—that is so childish. You know what a brahmin is?" Krishna said, "What do you mean by a brahmin?" He replied with a story.

When Alexander invaded India and fought with Porus, he won. When he entered the state, he saw excellent administration, the whole of the land was tidy, clean and well maintained, people were living happily. So he asked Porus, "Who is responsible for your administration?" Porus replied: "There was a brahmin prime minister, who was responsible for all this administration." Alexander said, "I would like to talk to him." Porus answered, "He resigned because we lost the war, and has gone to his village." Alexander responded, "Call him, nevertheless." So they sent a messenger who came back the next day with the response, "Tell the king I am no longer in his service. A brahmin does not go to anyone, therefore I am sorry that I cannot come." As this was narrated, Alexander said, "All right, I will go to his village."

Alexander was taken to the village, where the brahmin was seated under a tree teaching two children. When Alexander was announced, the man looked up and said, "Is there something I can do for you?" Alexander asked, "Are you the man who was the prime minister?" and the answer came, "Yes"; Alexander then said, "you ran an excellent administration," and the man responded, "Thank you". So Alexander asked him "Will you come with me? I will take you to Greece, give you a palace, make you the head of all our armies. Come with me!" the man considered this, looked up at Alexander, and replied, "Sorry, I want teach these children." Krishnamurti then said, "That's a brahmin—

somebody you can't buy, somebody who doesn't work for a reward. He did what was right for a brahmin to do: he ran as good an administration as he could. When he lost the war he took responsibility for the defeat and resigned, which is the right thing for the brahmins to do. When he was in the village, he did what he wanted to do, not in subservience to the king, or looking for some more rewarding job to do. That is the quality of the brahmin." After telling this story, K asked Krishna, "Now tell me, has the brahmin disappeared from this country?" I said, "I don't know, Sir, there may still be someone in the Himalayas, but I have not come across one."

On another occasion he asked Krishna, "Is there anything unique in this country anymore?" and Krishna said, "Maybe the family way of living, the affection with which people regard each other. But I can't say it is unique, because it exists elsewhere too, although perhaps not in the same measure." He nodded and kept quiet. He would often leave one with a question like that. Next day when Krishna met him he said, "Shall I tell you what is unique about this country? I have travelled all over the world, and I have watched. This is the only country left where the poor man still smiles." That is the kind of thing he noticed, not palaces, achievements, bridges, railway trains. He was watching the people, how they were living, and he saw that the poor man in India still smiles. The poor man in America or Europe feels wretched, deprived, but in India his spirit has not been destroyed in spite of the poverty. Then he added, "Although we are losing that quality in our country, it is still there."

These questions and comments become a source of tremendous learning if one dwells on them, takes them to heart, Krishna asserts. "He never wanted us to accept what he said but to reflect on it, ponder for ourselves, and see if it was true or not. One has to do the work for oneself. In all his life he never allowed anybody to use him as a crutch: he wanted no disciples, no help, he had a sense of renunciation. He gave his talks just out of affection."

So how does one describe such a consciousness? Krishna queries "Whatever one describes is so verbal, so inadequate, compared to what one wants to convey. It is not because he gave wonderful lectures; one can come across better speakers. One can even come across people who can explain his teachings more systematically. The ability to speak or lecture is trivial, although useful. It is what the consciousness is—the freedom, love and compassion in the consciousness that is precious. We are all fortunate to have had such a person amidst us. It does not matter whether we look upon him as a Theosophist or not, whether he left the Theosophical Society or not. Those are all trivial. A man like that does not belong to anybody, to the Krishnamurti Foundation, or the Theosophical Society. He does not belong to India but to the world. Ofcourse, he was born in a particular family, brought up and educated in some school. That school could take credit for having produced such a person, but was he this way because of the school, or in spite of it?

Achyut Patwardhan told Krishna once that the World Teacher was born in answer to the tears of the world. Therefore he belongs to humanity. Mrs. Besant had told Patwardhan, "When you find that you disagree with something that Krishnamurti said, never discard it, or ignore it, keep it in your mind. He is a superior consciousness, and when that says something we must reflect on it, not reject it". And this is what Patwardhan said: "I never rejected anything that Krishnaji said, however wrong it may have seemed to me. I dwelt on it."

What a great privilege for the Theosophical Society and for the Krishnamurti Foundation, Krishna comments, and for all who had the opportunity to interact with Krishnaji, to look after such a person, to publish his books, to make his teachings available to the world, or just to be with him, to know him. In this twentieth century it is very rare to find a man like that. Once when he was asked by someone, "Where do you come from?" he replied, "I come from the Valley of the Rishis"; and that is where he belongs, in the Valley of the Rishis.

Here is a narrative based on the recollections of Krishnamurti by Nadesan Satyendra, a writer from Sri Lanka: It was a cool December evening in Madras. The year was 1974. Nadesan Satyendra and his wife were visiting a friend in Egmore. Around 5 p.m., the friend said that he had to leave them to listen to a talk by Jiddu Krishnamurti at Adyar. He asked, "Why don't both of you come with me?". Satyendra was reluctant. He had attempted to read some of Krishnamurti's writings some ten years previously and had found him complex and difficult. He told his friend, "You go ahead, we will meet you again tomorrow". The friend's response was unexpected. He replied, "Next to my father, Krishnamurti is the man whom I love most. Why don't you come". The friend was what one may call a 'good man' — kind, sincere and helpful and it was more because of the regard that the Satyendras had for their friend than for Krishnamurti, that they went to Adyar that evening.

The Krishnamurti Centre at Adyar is set in spacious surroundings. The talk was scheduled to commence at 5 p.m. in the open air under a large spreading tree. There were about 300-400 persons gathered to hear Krishnamurti. Many were seated on the ground in front of the small raised dais reserved for the speaker. Behind those who were seated were a few rows of chairs. The Satyendras sat on the chairs and awaited Krishnamurti's arrival.

Sharp at 5 p.m., a small fair man with chiselled features, dressed in white, walked briskly to the raised platform, seated himself and began talking. There were no introductions. To this day, Satyendra has not forgotten Krishnamurti's first few words, "If you already know what I am going to say, you need not have come."

Satyendra was lounging in his chair. After all he had come because of his friend. But, at these words, he straightened myself and sat up. Krishnamurti's talk that evening was on the conditioned mind. He spoke about meditation and the control of thought. Who is the controller and who is the controlled? he asked. There was much that Satyendra saw for the first time that evening — it was like coming back to the beginning and knowing it for the first time. After that occasion, he heard Krishnamurti again, this time, in Colombo in 1978. He spoke of time. Thought is time, he said. Time was something that had always intrigued Satyendra. As a child, at the Galle Face Green in Colombo, he would watch with concern as ships disappeared in the curved horizon of the Indian Ocean. He wondered whether the ships had fallen off the edge. As he grew older, he learnt that the earth was not flat, that it was a globe, that there was no 'edge' and that the ships were safe.

But then, as he travelled back home from the Galle Face Green at night, seated in the rear seat of his father's small car, with his parents in front, he would look up at the sky at the distant stars and wonder what was there beyond the stars — and beyond that — and beyond that... He thought that though he did not know then, he would when he 'grew up'. When he 'grew up' the answer continued to elude him.

Later, he did learn something about Einstein's concept of curved space and the space—time continuum. He recognised that Einstein's mathematical equations explained certain physical phenomena, but he still could not 'see' curved space — this seemed to contradict everything that he had taken for granted in the three dimensional world — a three dimensional world with time somehow 'flowing' through it.

Of course, if space was 'curved', then it would have no beginning or end — and there would no 'edge' to fall off. Again, given a space—time continuum, there would be no beginning and end to time either. These he could conceptualise in his mind. Cause and effect would presumably merge in a space—time continuum. As Yogaswamy, the sage from Jaffna would often say in Tamil: "everything was over long, long ago."

He felt somewhat like Woody Allen in the film Annie Hall. A mournful looking Woody Allen is taken to the doctor. The doctor inquires cheerfully, "So what is the trouble, young man?". Woody Allen looks even more mournful and says, "The universe is expanding — and it will explode". Satyendra does not recall the exact words of the Doctor's response but the message was clear — "Stop wasting your time with stupid thoughts and get on with your life."

And, here Krishnamurti was quietly insisting that thought is time. Satyendra met Krishnamurti with a few friends on the morning after his lecture in Colombo. They were all seated on the carpeted floor. Satyendra asked Krishnamurti whether he would expand on that which he had said about time. K looked kindly at him, took his hands in his and started talking. It was almost like someone teaching a child to play table tennis by taking the child's hand together with the bat and showing him the feel of the stroke.

Perhaps Krishnamurti did not want to be quite as brutal as the Zen master who when asked by his pupil 'what is enlightenment' replied 'cowdung'. It is said that the pupil eventually recognised that the words of any teacher, however wise, as to what was enlightenment, would be like the dung that the cow excreted after chewing the cud.

A few months later, Satyendra participated as a panelist in a discussion meeting with Krishnaji at Adyar. A Tibetan monk was another participant. Satyendra says he particularly remembers the ending of the morning session. Krishnamurti had talked about the computer, artificial intelligence and the brain for about 20 minutes and as he finished, the entire audience (of about 100) fell into a deep silence — and the silence was pregnant.

In the silence, Satyendra was reminded of Krishnamurti's of—quoted statement: "Reality is the interval between two thoughts". The modern rationalist discourse founded on Descartes' search for certainty and the Cartesian conclusion "I think, therefore I am", seemed somehow far removed from reality. Irreverently, Satyendra thought of Peter Sellers in the film 'Party'. Sellers plays the role of an Indian and he is asked by someone: "Who do you think you are?". Sellers draws himself up to his full height, looks piercingly at the questioner and replies: "Sir, in India we do not think, we know who we are!"

Today, the so—called certainties of modernism are yielding to the more wholistic approach of the post—modern world. Many have begun to grasp the force of reason in Aurobindo's remarks: "The capital period of my intellectual development was when I could see clearly that what the intellect said might be correct and not correct, that what the intellect justified was true and its opposite was also true. I never admitted a truth in the mind without simultaneously keeping it open to the contrary of it. And the first result was that the prestige of the intellect was gone."

Krishnamurti's teachings were summarised with his approval, on 21 October 1980, in this way: "The core of Krishnamurti's teaching is contained in the statement he made in 1929 when he said: 'Truth is a pathless land'. Man cannot come to it through any organization, through any creed, through any dogma, priest or ritual, not through any philosophic knowledge or psychological technique. He has to find it through the mirror of relationship, through the understanding of the contents of his own mind, through observation and not through intellectual analysis or introspective dissection.

"Man has built in himself images as a fence of security, religious, political, personal. These manifest as symbols, ideas, beliefs. The burden of these images dominates man's thinking, his relationships and his daily life. These images are the causes of our problems for they divide man from man. His perception of life is shaped by the concepts already established in his mind. The content of his consciousness is his entire existence. This content is common to all humanity."

"The individuality is the name, the form and superficial culture he acquires from tradition and environment. The uniqueness of man does not lie in the superficial but in complete freedom from the content of his consciousness,which is common to all mankind. So he is not an individual.

"Freedom is not a reaction; freedom is not a choice. It is man's pretence that because he has choice he is free.

"Freedom is pure observation without direction, without fear of punishment and reward. Freedom is without motive; freedom is not at the end of the evolution of man but lies in the first step of his existence. In observation one begins to discover the lack of freedom. Freedom is found in the choiceless awareness of our daily existence and activity.

"Thought is time. Thought is born of experience and knowledge which are inseparable from time and the past. Time is the psychological enemy of man. Our action is based on knowledge and therefore time, so man is always a slave to the past. Thought is ever-limited and so we live in constant conflict and struggle. There is no psychological evolution.

"When man becomes aware of the movement of his own thoughts he will see the division between the thinker and thought, the observer and the observed, the experiencer and the experience. He will discover that this division is an illusion. Then only is there pure observation which is insight without any shadow of the past or of time. This timeless insight brings about a deep radical mutation in the mind.

"Total negation is the essence of the positive. When there is negation of all those things that thought has brought about psychologically, only then is there love, which is compassion and intelligence."

The last time that Satyendra met with Krishnamurti was in January 1984. He was in Madras and he went to hear him at Adyar. He was invited to join Krishnamurti at lunch on the following day. It was a simple vegetarian meal and there were four or five of them at the table. He told Krishnamurti that he had said something the previous evening and that he had not seen it quite in the same way before. He laughed.

Satyendra continued: 'You said that the 'I' was always in the past". Krishnamurti's eyes twinkled. He said: "It clicked, did it?"

Krishnamurti inquired about the July 1983 incidents in Sri Lanka and he was horrified to learn at first hand about some of the attacks and the resulting plight of the Tamil people. He had been thinking about visiting Sri Lanka at the end of the year but had decided against going. The conversation at the lunch table was easy and informal. Krishnaji spoke about his love for fast cars in the days of his youth. He related a joke about a Soviet astronaut. There was this Soviet astronaut, he said, who had gone to into space and returned to Moscow. The astronaut was feted by the Soviet people and the final reception before his world tour was held in the Kremlin. The Kremlin reception rooms, with their high domes, huge chandeliers and plush red carpets were packed to capacity. The Soviet President, Brezhnev took the astronaut to a quiet corridor and asked: "Tell me, when you went up there, did you see God?". The astronaut, looked around cautiously and replied in a whisper "Yes, I did." Brezhnev said: "I thought as much, but make certain that you do not tell anybody else about this."

Satyendra smiled and Krishnamurti went on. The astronaut left on his world tour and he was given grand receptions in Germany, in England and in the United States. The final reception of the world tour was in the Vatican in Rome.

The reception rooms in the Vatican with their high domes, huge chandeliers and plush red carpets were packed to capacity. The Pope invited the astronaut to a secluded corridor and asked: " Tell me, when you went up there, did you see God?"

The astronaut looked around cautiously, and remembering Brezhnev's command, replied: "No, I did not see God." The Pope said: "I thought as much, but please do not tell anybody else about this." All those at the table joined with Krishnamurti in the laughter. The conversation then turned to the possibility of Krishnamurti addressing the United Nations.

Krishnamurti looked at Satyendra and said: "Sir, if you were asked to address the United Nations, what would you say?". Satyendra was taken aback at the directness and suddenness of the query. He hesitated. He did not want to make a fool of himself — and appear presumptuous in his presence. He decided to take what appeared to me the cautious option. He replied: "Krishnaji, I do not think that I would have anything to say".

Krishnamurti's response was quick: "Does that mean that you have nothing to say?" And as I was trying to recover from the force of the body blow, Krishnamurthy delivered the knockout. He said: "Does that mean that you do not care?".

It was a learning process. My 'modesty' was shown up to be pretentious. Many years later in 1987, after the Indo — Sri Lanka Accord was signed, Satyendra was invited to speak in London on the Accord and its effect on the struggle for Tamil Eelam.

He commenced his talk by relating this story about Krishnamurti and went on to say: "I must confess that it was with some hesitation that I accepted the invitation to speak this evening. But as I reflected on that meeting with Krishnaji in Adyar, I was persuaded to accept because I cannot deny that I do care about what is happening to us as a people and because it would be wrong for me to say that I have nothing to say about the Tamil struggle and the Indo Sri Lanka Accord."

To Satyendra Jiddu Krishnamurti will always be the essential gnana yogi, the man who denied that he was a messiah but who spoke and wrote for more than fifty years thereafter, to ever growing audiences and who insisted to the end: "No man from outside can make you free... No one holds the Key to the Kingdom of Happiness. No one has the authority to hold that key. That key is your own self, and in the development and the purification and in the incorruptibility of that self alone is the Kingdom of Eternity...".

There has been extensive debate on the meaning and implications of the process that afflicted Krishnamurti since 1922. M. Bradford and P. Hayne of the Institute of Consciousness Research argue that the phenomenon represents the rising of the Kundalini. They base their argument on the testimony of Gopi Krishna who claims to have experienced the rising of the Kundalini in his own person. (Quoted by permission of M. Bradford)

The authors claim that "throughout the known history of mankind there have been individuals in every culture who have experienced a 'mystical' perception beyond the scope of normal human understanding. Each has tried in vain to express in comprehensible language the Reality that they have perceived and to deliver the message that this state of Being is our eventual destiny. Likewise the geniuses of the past and present present a puzzle to modern science to explain how it is that certain individuals can be so extraordinarily talented compared to their contemporaries."

They go on to say that Pandit Gopi Krishna, "expressed repeatedly his conviction that these trans—human states of mind are the outcome of a psycho-physiological mechanism in the human body, known from ancient times in India as Kundalini."

Gopi Krishna has given accounts of his own transformation, concluding that mankind is destined for a new, higher, expanded state of consciousness beyond anything which we can, at present, genuinely understand. He also felt that a critical examination of the lives of mystics and geniuses would provide a wealth of corroborative evidence for his theories and would be the starting point for a comprehensive scientific investigation of Kundalini as the mechanism of human evolution.

The authors take this cue to examine Krishnamurti in the light of Gopi Krishna's theories. The Theosophical Society selected Krishnamurti as the vehicle for the World

Teacher on the basis of his aura which reputedly 'was entirely free of selfishness'.

"But in 1921, at the age of 26," the authors write, "he had an experience which irreversibly altered the course of his life." He began questioning the activities of the T.S. until in 1929 and broke away from it.

What happened in August of 1921? Krishnamurti began "to experience extreme pain at the nape of his neck where a lump-like muscle spasm had appeared. The next morning, he seemed to fall into a semi-conscious state, characterized by fits of moaning and restlessness and accompanied by extreme internal heat. These states alternated with periods of relatively normal consciousness in which he became tranquil, generally at meal times. His digestive system tended to reject most of the food that was fed to him, but he slept at night as usual. This continued for three days with his consciousness becoming more and more intermittent and the fits and heat intensifying. He had become unbearably sensitive and even the most minute physical sounds upset him terribly. On the evening of the third day, he went through an experience which is best described in an account which he wrote two days later:

'I felt myself going out of my body. I saw myself sitting down with the delicate tender leaves of the tree over me. I was facing the east. In front of me was my body and over my head I saw the Star, bright and clear. Then I could feel the vibrations of the Lord Buddha . . . . I was so happy, calm and at peace. I could still see my body and I was hovering near it. There was such profound calmness both in the air and within myself, the calmness of the bottom of a deep unfathomable lake. Like the lake, I felt my physical body, with its mind and emotions, could be ruffled on the surface but nothing, nay nothing could disturb the calmness of my soul. The Presence of the mighty Beings was with me for some time and then They were gone. I was supremely happy, for I had seen. Nothing could ever be the same. I have drunk at the clear and pure waters at the source of the fountain of life and my thirst was appeased. Never more could I be thirsty, never more could I be in utter darkness; I have seen the Light. I have touched compassion which heals all sorrow and suffering; it is not for myself, but for the world. I have stood on the mountaintop and gazed at the mighty Beings. Never can I be in utter darkness; I have seen the glorious and healing Light. The fountain of Truth has been revealed to me and the darkness has been dispersed. Love in all its glory has intoxicated my heart; my heart can never be closed. I have drunk at the fountain of Joy and eternal Beauty. I am God-intoxicated.'

The authors contend that this testimony implies the rising of the Kundalini in Krishnamurti. They quote Dr. R.M. Bucke who in his Cosmic Consciouness listed characteristics which appear to be common, to a varying extent, to individuals experiencing cosmic consciousness. These criteria have been further elaborated by Gopi Krishna along with detailed physiological aspects of the condition so that a comprehensive set of criteria can now be used for evaluating individual experiences.

The authors proceed to evaluate Krishnamurti's accounts and those of his acquaintances in the light of these criteria.

Intellectual Elevation

Intellectual elevation is a clear feature, according to the authors, of the transformations occasioned by an aroused Kundalini. They point out that in his childhood and youth, Krishnamurti was a such a poor student as to be despair of some of his tutors, one of whom referred to him as 'particularly dim-witted'. He was even caned for his apparent refusal to learn. Yet, the authors point out, "many who read his books today agree that they are thought-provoking and profound" and go on to quote Anne Morrow Lindbergh who said about his book, *The First and Last Freedom,* "The reader is given in one paragraph, even in one sentence, enough to keep him exploring, questioning, thinking for days."

They also point out that from 1926 to 1931 Krishnamurti wrote sixty poems. He also gave innumerable talks worldwide, published dozens of books and founded eight schools. "Hardly the outcome for one characterized as 'particularly dim-witted'. It is evident from the accounts of those who knew him from an early age that Krishnamurti's capacity for comprehension and expression changed markedly after his experience in 1921," they conclude.

The Process

Not enough attention has been paid by modern students of the Kundalini to the physical and biological aspects of the phenomenon, something that Gopi Krishna stresses. Krishnamurti suffered from intermittent periods of pain in the neck and spine accompanied by mental symptoms, which he characterised as 'The Process', "a name which suggests that he was aware of a purposeful, controlled activity going on in his body," the authors argue.

Years later, they point out, the pain was accompanied by other feelings; "Several times, after sleeping, he woke with a sense of special joy, feeling that the room was full of 'eminent holy beings' . . . .and he felt, as always at such times, that something was happening to his brain, expanding it." Krishnamurti writes, "the body does not resist or protest against the pain . . .There is an unknown energy involved in all this." And later again; "But there was an activity deep within which was wearing out all obstructions."

Additionally he says; "Deep inside me I know what has happened. I have been stocked with gasoline. The tank is full." And also, "The purification of the brain is necessary. Only when the brain has cleansed itself of its conditioning, greed, envy, ambition, then only can it comprehend that which is complete. Love is that completeness."

Inner Light

The authors consider an 'illuminated' mental perception as probably the single most definitive feature of mystical experience, "because the perception of internal light has been mentioned repeatedly by countless mystics throughout history... The accounts of the experience of the 'Inner Light' made by Krishnamurti and others suggests that the mental processes become powered by an as yet undetectable, luminous energy."

Psychic Gifts

The authors reason that psychic gifts like healing and clairvoyance that have been attributed to Krishnamurti suggest the action of an evolutionary super-intelligent life-force. Krishnamurti himself, however, tended to dismiss the importance of such faculties, though he did not deny them. "Perhaps he felt that such an ability was not an end in itself, but rather a distraction from real spiritual development, and also that it could be an intrusion upon others' privacy," the authors argue. "He emphasised throughout his teaching that internal personal growth is far more important than the development of psychic abilities."

Compassion

The authors point to Krishnamurti's widely testified compassionate nature and to his ability to empathise with his interlocutor particularly in private. In public he sounded much more distant.

Personal Magnetism

A powerful personal magnetism was a strong characteristic exhibited by Krishnamurti on most of those who met and knew him, drawing large audiences wherever he went a characteristic he shares with those in whom the Kundalini is active, according to the authors.

Expanded Consciousness

The authors quote copiously from *Krishmamurti's Journal, Notebooks* and other atterances to prove that he shared an expanded cosmic consciousness with the world's well-known mystics.

Religious Impulse

"Dr. R. M. Bucke claimed quite emphatically, as did Gopi Krishna, that religious desire would, upon the awakening to higher consciousness, bloom into a conviction, a spiritual realization, a new perception which surpasses our present concepts of Reality, Self and Creator," the authors argue. "Krishnamurti experienced much of this and it runs throughout his teachings. Perhaps he had lost his sense of aloneness or separateness and gained a unity with something greater, yet unexplainable."

They quote an excerpt from a talk he gave in 1928 which summarizes in part his early view on religious striving. "I hold that there is an eternal life which is the Source and the Goal, the beginning and the end, and yet it is without end or beginning. In that Life alone is there fulfilment. And anyone who fulfils that Life has the key to Truth without limitation. That Life is for all. Into that Life the Buddha, the Christ entered. From my point of view I have attained, I have entered into that Life. That Life has no form as Truth has no form, no limitation. And to that Life, everyone must return."

Sense of Immortality

The authors quote Krishnamurti on immortality in a statement made in1935; "Now I can say there is immortality, to me it is a personal experience, the mind must free itself from the habit of self-protecting acquisition; when it is utterly naked, then there is immortality." They observe that these comments are all the more significant when it is noted that often Krishnamurti's health was bad. He many times fainted and at other times his energy seemed to be all but completely drained. The pain of the 'process' on some occasions persisted for weeks, and yet he was absolutely certain that the spirit was indestructible.

Mystical Perception

Perhaps the most dramatic and compelling evidence of the

development of the cosmic sense, in the authors' view is the "mystical perception and the ecstasy which accompanies it. Krishnamurti gives us some examples of his inner and outer experience in the Notebook:

" . . . what took place was beyond all words and description. It was the center of all creation; it was a purifying seriousness that cleansed the brain of every thought, and feeling; its seriousness was as lightning which destroys and burns up; the profundity of it was not measurable, it was there immovable, impenetrable, a solidity that was as light as the heavens . . . There was only seeing, the eyes that saw beyond time-space.

". . .of a sudden, that unknowable immensity was there, not only in the room and beyond but also deep, in the innermost recesses, which was once the mind . . . that immensity left no mark, it was there, clear, strong, impenetrable and unapproachable whose intensity was fire which left no ash. With it was bliss."

"Suddenly one felt this immense flame of power . . . It is beyond all thought and words to describe what's going on, the strangeness of it and the love, the beauty of it. It's beyond and above all faculties of man."

Krishnamurti hints at the brain's part in this, "The brain had lost all its responses; it was only an instrument of observation, it was seeing, not as the brain belonging to a particular person but as a brain which is not conditioned by time-space . . ." And also, "All this seemed to affect the brain; it was not as it was before. Because of it, relationships seem to have changed. As a terrific storm, a destructive earthquake gives a new course to the rivers, changes the landscape . . . so it has levelled the contours of thought, changed the shape of the heart.

The Product of Illumination

If illumination, the authors aver, is the goal of human evolution, then the attributes of one blessed with it will be a gift and a blessing to all humanity. Whether it is poetry, music, science or healing, the expression in some way will enhance our civilization. This is true in the case of Jiddu Krishnamurti. A few quotes from observers give an impression of the impact he made on audiences. The Times Literary Supplement said, "The insight, spiritual and poetical, of these commentaries is as simply expressed as it is searching in its demands." The author Francis Hackett wrote in New Republic; "I feel that he has hold of a major secret." In The Observer, his second book *The First and Last Freedom* was acclaimed: "For those who wish to listen it will have value beyond words." Mary Lutyens says; "I find I understand him with that sense, that intuition, which grasps the meaning of difficult poetry, rather than through my intellect."

Krishnamurti always maintained that he did not rehearse his teaching. "It is like, what is the biblical term? Revelation. It happens all the time when I'm talking. This simple person Krishnamurti has not come to the teaching through thought."

This too suggests that the talks, the talents of Krishnamurti are not just his but are for all who listen. At the core of his teaching is the message that 'profound psychological transformation' is the aim of his teaching and the goal of each life. "Liberation—each individual must hold a mirror to his own consciousness and strive to develop freedom. There is a direct line to Truth within each individual."

Other Factors

The authors claim that a "marked feature of Krishnamurti's life was his lack of physical relationships with women. Although many of them fell in love with him, he seemed to have no need for the physical expression of sex and, in the first half of his life, even had a strong aversion to it. It would seem that the sexual energy was primarily directed upwards and was used entirely for the evolution of the brain and nervous system." They were obviously unaware of his relationship with Rosalind Rajagopal, which was disclosed after his death.

In summary, the authors draw two conclusions,

1) "we have seen that Krishnamurti's experiences conform to many of the criteria outlined above. But, although he seemed to display some of the features of expanded consciousness, it is evident from his accounts that the condition was not perennial, that is, a permanently functioning feature of his awareness.The development of the nervous system to the point where the cosmic sense is completely functional is, it would seem, a very, very rare occurrence."

2) "Another main feature of full enlightenment, that is, the revelation of new knowledge which more clearly defines the direction the race must take in its evolutionary development, is there to perhaps a lesser degree. His advice to individuals concerning the transcendence of the normal thinking patterns is not an entirely new idea in the history of spiritual teaching. When questioned about the source of his knowledge and the mechanism by which he manifested it, he was at a loss to explain it. Thus, the physiological and other scientific aspects of his experiences, necessary for a clear understanding of the phenomenon, are to a large degree absent from his teachings."

How would Krishnamurti have reacted to this analysis? There is little doubt that he would have dubbed it a product of thought which is really irrelevant to the understanding of the Immeasurable as he termed it.

Krishnamurti and Theosophy: Full Circle?

The relations between Krishnamurti and the Theosophical Society have undergone a circular development, from adulation of Krishnamurti by the Theosophists, to their rejection by Krishnamurti and finally an apparent mutual accommodation by both. Various perceptions by various factions in Theosophy are discernible over the years in their various literary productions. Aryel Sanat, a noted modern Theosophist and author of *The Inner Life of J.Krishnamurti*, (Quest Books) wrote on Krishnamurti and Transformation, a chapter in his *Secret Doctrine, Krishnamurti and Transformation.* "When Krishnamurti came on the theosophical scene," Sanat notes, "the universal understanding in all the theosophical and other new age organizations was that theosophy—or the perennial philosophy under whatever other name—is primarily a metaphysical system, a logical construct of concepts and ideas. It was thought (and still is) that theosophy consists of a series of teachings that, in their reasonableness, lead human beings to live the spiritual life, which was understood as following a number of set rules.

Nevertheless, a careful perusal of all the original sources (the letters from the Masters, H. P. Blavatsky's writings, and the writings of some of the *chelas*) shows that the real teaching was never meant to be merely a "rational" exposition of "reality." Rather, it was presented first and foremost as a series of intuitive injunctions and exhortations to inspire interest in the life of transformation, the life of brotherhood and unconditional acceptance of that which is the case... As was pointed out by Master KH to Mrs. Besant, "No one has a right to claim authority over a pupil or his conscience. Ask him not what he believes... The crest wave of intellectual advancement must be taken hold of and guided into Spirituality. It cannot be forced into beliefs and ceremonial worship."

Thus, Sanat writes, the presence of Krishnamurti in the midst of the theosophical world can then be perceived as not having been a mistake nor a bizarre coincidence. "It was through Krishnamurti that the first lesson of the teaching of Shambhala was spotlessly given to the world at large. What he spoke of throughout his life addressed the necessity for dying from moment to moment (in the theosophical terminology, the death of the personality). He further addressed the problem of our not being able to understand, to really "know," anything, so long as perception comes from conditioning, from a point of view."

The life of concepts and conditioning, Sanat continues, is clearly also the life of the personality, of the conditioned mind, so (again, putting it in theosophical terms) he was pointing to the need to allow something other than the personality to determine our understanding of things. But he absolutely refused to give a name to that "other" that came about when the conditioned mind is not there, such as is done in some theosophical, Hindu and Buddhist schools. This refusal of his baffled many, who demanded to be given a "rational" picture of the world... Whenever words are used to refer to this "other" beyond the conceptual mind, everything is thereby relegated to the plane of the conditioned mind, no matter how "profound" or "spiritual" it may sound, Sanat points out.

That teaching proposes, Sanat says, that the beginning of learning takes place with the death of the conditioned mind—and with it of all concepts.

Krishnamurti showed uncompromisingly what a serious and dangerous mistake it is to categorize sublime notions, according to Sanat. Anyone who only believes in "the oneness of life," for instance, and is not actually existing in the state of being all life, is thereby almost certain to be falling asleep and going astray from the life of transformation, in which there can be no such concept. It may very well be that, upon the actual dying of the conditioned mind with all its concepts and conditionings, there may come the discovery that life is one, after all. But that also is a very dangerous idea to pursue, because that sort of speculation is but another conceptual distraction from the life of transformation.

Consequently, in Sanat's view, Krishnamurti's presence in the 20th Century has made it possible for each of us to have a real litmus test for how serious we actually are about theosophy, about that which is. It implies that a theosophist is not necessarily someone who holds certain beliefs, but rather someone who lives the life of transformation. Another implication in all this is that anyone who believes in or presents theosophy to others as if it were a series of fixed teachings, would be, despite good intentions, most lamentably misrepresenting the truth, and possibly doing a disservice to the esoteric teaching.

Sanat tries to show in his book that there is a very clear and incontestable intimate relationship between the Kalachakra lineage, Nagarjuna and Zen, the Masters who began the theosophical movement, the teaching of the perennial philosophy, the Secret Doctrine, and Krishnamurti. However, this need not mean that Krishnamurti (or the Masters, for that matter) need be accepted ao*priori* as a supreme authority in spiritual matters.

Authority, after all, he says, can be seen to be but another concept of the conditioned mind—accepted or rejected according to its prejudices—so anyone who follows authorities is not likely to be living the life of transformation. It is the conditioned mind that arbitrarily creates the notions of the "superior" and the "inferior," so indispensable for having authorities. But in reality, such distinctions have absolutely no meaning.

Krishnamurti, Sanat maintains, was not an authority, in part precisely because he can now be seen to have been an integral part of a much larger picture—of a Tibetan t'angka scroll painting, one might say, created in Shambhala.

Another noted Theosophist was Geoffrey Hodson who had changing views on Krishnamurti. Some of them are described in his *Krishnamurti and the Search for Light*, written in the 1930s.

"Krishnamurti has undoubtedly brought a measure of life and light to the world," Hodson admits. "He achieves this largely by concentrating upon one aspect of life and light. He is obviously inspired with a passion for original thought and a scorn for the repetition of accepted formula. For him, tradition is anathema, the wisdom of the ages a delusion and a snare. He sees truly that humanity will never be wise, and therefore happy, until the individual thinks for himself, stands upon his own intellectual, emotional and physical feet. His message would appear to be 'discover truth for yourself and by yourself.' He seems either to be unaware of or deliberately to ignore the fact that without detailed guidance the majority of men are totally incapable of self-illumination."

Krishnamurti himself is uniquely individual in his views, Hodson goes on. He delves deep into his own consciousness in search of the solution of life's problems.

He refuses to be guided, apparently in order to preserve the clarity of his own perception. He is an apostle of the virgin mind, the white mental sheet, the new beginning. He advocates a ruthless cutting adrift from the past. He tells us to ignore the future and be acutely focussed in the present. He wants us to live our own lives to the full, making the very most of every moment. We are to accept life's experiences, give ourselves fully yet impersonally over to them, and so realise their sublime significance.

Hodson holds that Krishnamurti is the personification of simple mindedness. He is sincerity incarnate, and is clearly inspired with a selfless desire to lead humanity to its own light. He concentrates on individual self-knowledge, individual perfection and enlightenment. Up to now he has seemed to ignore, even to deny, the value of the path of action, of deliberate self-training, study and ministration to the world. Unfortunately, Hodson maintains, he proclaims his to be the only way and the equally certain and most glorious path of selfless service an illusion, a way of cowardice, of escape from reality. In him, singleness of purpose has developed into intolerance. Unique individuality has become a fetish, worship of which produces narrow-mindedness and causes him to display distinct signs of intellectual arrogance. He alone is right. Everyone else, from the Lord Buddha down to the latest teacher of the Law, is wrong, criminally wrong.

Thus it would appear, Hodson concludes, that Krishnamurti is human, though in some respects above the majority of men. He has achieved the heights, and this makes the more injurious his descents into the vale. Perceiving the altitudes, those whom he influences do not always discriminate between them and the valleys, between truth and error. This is unfortunate, for one of the marked characteristics of his teaching is its unevenness, its variability.

Let us be inspired with the hope that Krishnamurti will ascend to even greater heights as a teacher and remain thereon, Hodson asserts. "For he is a great man with a great message as yet but partially delivered. We are in a most critical period of world history. We need Krishnamurti who possesses that genius, those rare qualities which make a leader and a saviour of the world."

In his book Hodson comments upon Krishnamurti's teachings. He pays homage to the truth which he has been able to perceive in them. He challenges those utterances which appear to him erroneous, and on occasion he advances certain theosophical ideas.

1. Enquiry

Hodson claims that Krishnamurti's utterances are an extraordinary blend of rare flashes of transcendental wisdom, penetrating intelligence, incomprehensibility, prejudice, intolerance and vituperation. In offering some thoughts upon his various teachings, he says, he is moved to do so partly because after arrival in Australia he became aware of the influence of the teachings of Krishnamurti upon the membership of The Theosophical Society. One Lodge had just sustained severe losses in the resignation of some of its most talented and promising students.

In addition, the most prominent workers in The Theosophical Society had received in silence the continuous and vituperative denunciations of Krishnamurti. They could afford to be silent knowing that truth is certain to prevail and falsehood to be exposed.

Hodson confesses, however, that "as a member of the Society, I have not always been able to achieve the philosophic calm of the leaders. The principles of justice, fair play and common courtesy have been so flagrantly outraged for some seven years that at last I am moved to a reply. I have kept in touch with Krishnamurti's teachings, attending his gatherings when possible, and reading his published addresses. In Australia I also sought an opportunity of learning direct by what line of thought these ex-members had arrived at the conclusion that Theosophy was valueless, was indeed a hindrance in the process of self-illumination and the fulfilment of life. I sought first those truths in the teachings of Krishnamurti which had proved so enlightening. Second, I wanted to know in what way these truths differ from or are outside of Theosophy. Third, and perhaps most important, I desired to discover why one must discard Theosophy, self-purification, study and service, must resign from all movements and give up all good work in order to receive enlightenment. These for me have been important questions for some years."

Two long sessions of exposition and question and answer with one ex-fellow of the Theosophical Society who, following Krishnamurti, had resigned from various organisations, failed completely to convey one single idea to which Hodson's mind could wholly assent, saying: "this is a great truth, and one, moreover, which is outside of Theosophy." A genuine mutual liking existed between Hodson's informant and himself, and the occasion seemed to be the most promising he had yet found; for here was one who was willing to analyse, to be questioned freely, frankly, and one moreover who, by theosophical study and self-training, was accustomed to logical processes of thought.

The first statement with which Hodson was confronted was "that there is no purpose in life." Seeking confirmation, he was informed that experience does not teach us anything. This is true to the doctrine of Krishnamurti, who positively affirms that there is no purpose even in suffering. The next statement was that liberation was for all, at whatever stage in the life-process they happened to stand, whether dustman or University professor, primitive man or genius. All could achieve immediate and complete self-fulfilment if they would. "Why do they not do so?" Hodson says he naturally asked. "Because they don't want to," was the reply. "Why do they not want to?" Hodson asked. "Because they have not had enough experience." "Then experience has a value?"

So there we were, Hodson comments, in the first of a succession of closed circles of thought, of contradictions from which, despite my every endeavour, it was impossible to escape. Eventually, because of this, the discussions were discontinued. Hodson's friend frankly confessed his inability to present to him a logical case. He said that his perpetual challenge of every inconsistency and contradiction rendered exposition of Krishnamurti's ideas impossible. He said that you have to take a very great deal which appears incomprehensible and illogical and hold it in your mind without immediate rejection if you would understand.

Hodson replied that such confusion of thought, such housing of mental concepts against which reason and intuition utterly rebel would plunge him into a kind of a hell of mental confusion. Since suffering is said to be purposeless, Hodson was not prepared to go so far. It was clear to him that, like many in the same position, his friend was himself experiencing mental darkness and anguish. As a result of cutting himself off from his friends, his life work and his highest ideals of human conduct, as so many others have done at the bidding of Krishnamurti, he found himself in misery and loneliness. He admitted this, and said that Krishnamurti taught that it was necessary to pass through this stage in order to achieve discernment. Hodson could not forbear to say: "And yet experience is valueless and life has no purpose?" Happily with friendship unaffected, they were constrained to leave the matter there.

This experience would appear to be not uncommon, Hodson comments. At Ojai, a questioner asked Krishnamurti, "Do you not see, sir, that your ideas can lead us but to one result—the blankness of negation and ineffectiveness in our struggle with the problems of life?" Hodson does not say what Krishnamurti replied nor does he say why he did not confront Krishnamurti himself since he attended his talks.

Similar confusion has arisen for many others who heroically have essayed the same path through negation and self-isolation in pursuance of the theme enunciated by Krishnamurti, Hodson maintains. But he wants to make it clear that he is not judging the case. He says he does not feel competent to do so. Such heroism may produce heroic results, he comments, despite the fact that Krishnamurti constantly warns against any course of conduct with a view to attainment, and quotes Krishnamurti's words on the subject: "When we understand profoundly the significance of our existence, of the process of ignorance and action, we will see what we call purpose has no significance. The mere search for the purpose of life covers up, detracts from the comprehension of oneself."

That quotation, Hodson maintains, is a perfect example of the closed circle of thought outside of which he for one continually finds himself to be shut when endeavouring to comprehend these teachings. For the opening clause, "When we understand profoundly the significance of our existence," he says, is for him the end, not the beginning of the search. This phenomenon is constant throughout all Krishnamurti's expositions. He seems to Hodson to put the very goal itself as the first step towards its attainment. "If I may presume to say so," Hodson offers, "of one so much greater than myself, he does not appear to appreciate the enormous gulf between himself as a very great and illuminated being and the rest of humanity in which he appears to be trying to initiate the process of thinking for itself. Krishnamurti himself apparently finds little or no favourable response from those whom he addresses. Evidently they find, as I do myself, their existent mental equipment unequal to the task of following the exceedingly abstruse concepts of which his talks are presumed to be expositions."

Hodson gives the example of a question put to him in various forms more than once: "I have listened to your talks for several years, but to be frank, I have not yet grasped what you are trying to convey." The answer, as usual, is itself as unacceptable (to Hodson, as he himself says) as the teachings which produced the question. Krishnamurti says, "All that I am trying to do is to help you to discern for yourself that there is no salvation outside of yourself, that no Master, no society can save you." Obviously that is not all he is trying to tell us; for such a statement is to be found in every one of the world religions and philosophies, and especially is it part of the central message of the one society which Krishnamurti has singled out as the chief target for his arrows of criticism and iconoclasm—The Theosophical Society.

What is wrong? Who is at fault, if fault there be? Are we not expected to understand? Is the whole purpose to throw us into a profound mental confusion out of which enlightenment will emerge? Hodson queries. "For Krishnamurti, the whole world and, therefore, his audiences, his questioners, and especially 'the continually vilified leaders and members of the Theosophical Society all these are wrong, are knaves and fools, whilst he alone is right. At least, so he continually seems to suggest."

What is to be done about this? Hodson queries and can find but one answer: We must bring the best powers of heart and mind to bear upon Krishnamurti's teaching. We must respect his greatness, and approach his message; even if he denies that he has one; without bias, or, if possible, with a leaning towards his way of thought. He himself demands much more. He says that one must discard every opinion, every belief, all knowledge wrested from life, throw overboard every experience however lofty, beautiful, ennobling and profound. For all these are contemptuously dismissed by him as superstitious beliefs, self-deceits and ways of escape from reality. As long as we hold to one single idea which life has made true for us we cannot know the truth. We must become mentally virginal. We must render our minds like a white sheet. Then, perhaps, but certainly not till then, a faint glimmer of light may dawn upon us.

Since Krishnamurti so greatly stresses it, Hodson proceeds to examine this concept of self-denudation. Students of the Ancient Wisdom know full well, he maintains, that two major psychological changes quite naturally both precede and accompany illumination. They consist first of psychological simplification, and second of self-unification, or the fusion of hitherto separated aspects of human nature into a unit. As a result of the first change, personal desire gradually disappears. The individual "wants" no more. Emotionally and intellectually he becomes independent of externals, for he has found a well-spring of life, of happiness and of truth within himself. His feelings become pure, white, still. His intellect is free of supposition, free of doubt, "simple," calm, direct. His mind, freed from a confusion of externally imposed creeds, dogmas and beliefs, is established in recognition of; not obsession by; certain basic metaphysical formula which have become for him the keys of life, his theosophia. The second change of self-unification, or the fusion of emotion and intellect into a single centre of awareness and action quite naturally accompanies this.

Clear-minded and unified, the individual has symbolically become "as a little child." If one understands Krishnamurti rightly, says Hodson he insists on bringing this condition about by force, artificially as it were. There must be positive action to eject all previous concepts of life. "When we begin to free ourselves, through experiment, from these false divisions with their special significances, pursuits and ideals, which have caused so much harm and falsely complicated our lives, then we shall release creative energy and discover the endless movement of life."

Hodson's own view of this self-clarification is that it is entirely a natural process; it is the result of interior changes, of the unfoldment of the life within. It is, therefore, not forced. Indeed, it seems doubtful whether it can be brought about artificially. Rather is it an inevitable occurrence, utterly spontaneous, perfectly natural, even thoughtless, or, at any rate, thought-free. Tagore beautifully expresses the spontaneity of this change in his words: "He who can open the bud, does it so simply."

Perhaps the most phenomenal concomitant of this condition of spiritual "budding" is its physical result, according to Hodson. The *karma* of material adversity begins to be outworn. In consequence, although no direct effort is ever made to obtain even the necessities of physical life, the "new-born" is never in need. All his wants are supplied, sometimes in abundance. Symbolically, the kings of the earth unite to lay their treasures at the Christ Child's feet.

What remains after this interior death and rebirth? Hodson queries and answers: That which remains is the individual centre of awareness. But the word "individual" does not imply separated individuality. For one of the great experiences which follow the process of denudation is the progressive fading of the sense of separateness. A state of unity with all is entered, first, in exhilarating flashes, and later as a permanent condition of consciousness. This individual centre of consciousness, this sublimated selfhood, displays three attributes or powers; those of intuition, reason and will. Intuition and reason are gradually fused into one, and they, with the fruit of their combined activity, remain as constituent attributes of the new-born Self. The third attribute of the Self consists of an awakened and burning will to know, to ascend, to conquer. This arises from fathomless depths within the centre of existence. Its presence and activity is experienced as a continuous and mounting determination to break all fetters, pierce all resistance to its own free, full and perfect manifestation.

Once awakened, Hodson maintains, this state never sleeps. Although its decrees may not always be ratified in action, especially at first, such temporary frustration has no effect upon it. Ever the will to victory mounts to become the one increasing purpose of life, the one exalting power. Though concentrated at burning-glass intensity in the individual, this will is known by him as impersonal, universal and in this resides its potency. Unconquerable and undiminished, pertaining to eternity, it becomes the fiery centre upon which individual existence is established.

Thus the One Will crowns, completes the three-fold centre of awareness in man which remains when all else has been "slain." Intuition, reason and the intellectual light — which is the result of their blended activity—these, fused in and empowered by the fire of will, these remain. Krishnamurti appears to carry this process very much further, in Hodson's view. Apparently the very thought of an ideal, a quest or any purpose in life is anathema to him. One in whom the awakening of the will to fulfilment has begun, who sees the goal of liberation before him and is moving deliberately towards it, cannot possibly comply with his demand for interior emptiness, agnosticism as an essential to illumination.

As to will-consciousness Krishnamurti says little, according to Hodson. But he does demand as an essential to illumination, at least as a result of listening to him, the complete ejection from the centre of awareness of all memory and all the distilled essence of the fruits of life's experiences. Apparently everything must go, and, moreover, the future is mortgaged. In his own words: "When a man says, 'I know,' he is dead." As Hodson interprets it, "One must neither remember one's own past nor be interested in one's future. One must not admit of or answer to interior illumination outside of his views, and one must not employ reason when listening to him. Apparently one must listen with empty, actionless mind and purposeless will. At least, that is the impression I receive when listening to him or reading his utterances. This negation appears to me to be implicit if not fully expressed. For if one does apply reason to certain of his teachings one must reject them as illogical and unsound. His denunciation of Theosophy as untrue, as poison, and, by implication, of a person like his 'mother,' Dr. Besant, as an exploiter of the people, is an example. This denunciation is impossible of acceptance by any individual who has studied and tested against life the one and has truly comprehended the other. To deny the Ancient Wisdom to a mind illuminated by it is comparable to denial of the existence and value of the sun to forms which derive from it their life and energy. For, throughout all ages the Ancient Wisdom has been as the sun to the unfolding mind of man. Yet Krishnamurti does deny the Ancient Wisdom albeit in terms which suggest that he knows little or nothing of its true light, its profundity and its beauty." Hodson goes on to quote Krishnamurti to support his conclusion: "... Schools of thought are nothing but imitative jargons which merely create divisions and encourage exclusiveness and vanity of mind. These systems of thought have really no validity, being founded on illusion."

Hodson comments that Dr. Besant was one of the greatest women and greatest servants of humanity of this age, and one moreover who dearly loved and deeply reverenced

Krishnamurti. In the face of his denial of Theosophy and his denunciation of Dr. Besant, both intuition and reason, stimulated by moral indignation, forbid either positive acceptance or empty-mindedness.

2. Test

In the first section of his analysis Hodson opened a discussion on the teachings of Krishnamurti. He frankly confessed that, in common, apparently, with large numbers of others, he has found himself unable to accept many of those teachings. He even went so far as to suggest that the extraordinary confusion of thought which he is causing everywhere he goes might be producing great harm.

Hodson believes that the majority of Krishnamurti's hearers and supporters are, or were, Fellows of the Theosophical Society. They are people who have at least some background of philosophic thought. They know what liberation, the one Life, the Life—force, mind-heart, the "I" consciousness may be presumed to mean. One would think that this knowledge would help them in understanding, both his use of such terms and his purpose in travelling continuously about the world.

Krishnamurti thinks otherwise, according to Hodson. He constantly affirms that the background, the process of study, the effort to understand the meaning and purpose of life which Theosophy inculcates—all these are a positive hindrance to the attainment of true discernment. Hodson claims to have often wondered what his words can mean to those of his listeners who have no background whatever, who have given no consideration to the concepts implied by the words referred to above. Do they experience a greater or a lesser confusion of mind than that of the theosophist listener? Is it possible that the very virginal state of their mentality is an advantage to them? Hodson queries. This is a point upon which enlightenment would be valuable. For it cannot be denied that one who has had certain definite experiences which have profoundly changed for the better his whole life cannot accept affirmations which positively deny both the experience and its source.

Let us take for example the question of direct experience of the immortality of the Soul, or, as it is put theosophically, causal consciousness, Hodson proposes. When this comes, whether as a result of meditation or as a sudden exaltation, the problem of the life after death is instantly and finally solved. The Self is known as undying and indestructible. It is also known as completely distinct from the body. Denials of the existence of such a centre of awareness and of such an experience can make no impression upon those who have known the one and have passed through the other. They are impervious to a teacher who does deny either the possibility or the value of such a basic experience.

Take, again, the question of help received as a result of joining a society, a church for example, Hodson suggests. "I personally passed through an experience at my confirmation as a schoolboy which profoundly influenced me at the time and still is a living power in my life. All that was highest and best in me was then strengthened, all that was undesirable was weakened. Though I may be far from having fully lived up to the experience, it has been of the greatest value to me, particularly in great trials and temptations. This experience is renewed for me every time I receive Holy Communion. I rise from the Lord's Table uplifted, refreshed spiritually and with my mind clarified and unusually alert. I therefore love the Christian Church and its Sacraments. I am profoundly grateful to the Church for this and similar experiences which it has helped to bring to me. Whilst admitting the evils of priestcraft, I can never assent to the wholesale condemnation of religions, churches and priests to which Krishnamurti gives expression. I know of many noble and splendid men in the priesthood, and I know of the value of their lives to those who come into contact with them. I also know that very great numbers of people have had exaltations, spiritual reorientation and self-correction through participation in the services and Sacraments of the Christian Church."

Such people would be false to the very highest within themselves, Hodson asserts, would be traitors to a spiritual principle, if they gave assent to the denials and fulminations of a religious iconoclast. It is neither just nor fair to ask or expect them to do so. Particularly is it unfair to condemn them and even indict them as exploiters, and to class them and the whole body of the priesthood with all the most evil people in the world. Yet this is what Krishnamurti continually does.

Take also the question of the existence of the Masters of the Wisdom and the value of the experience of communion with one or more of Them and of becoming an agent for Their superior powers, Hodson suggests. The individual for whom this is a reality is at a distinct disadvantage when trying to understand Krishnamurti. For not only does he constantly condemn the whole concept of the discipleship, but he also says that "discernment" is impossible to one for whom such an association is a living fact. He seems to impute a selfish motive to everyone concerned in the experience. He seems also to think that anyone who accepts the idea of the Masters does so solely because a "leader" has told him to do so. He appears to reject entirely the possibility of any direct experience. The Masters Themselves and all Their senior pupils are exploiters and all other disciples and aspirants are voluntarily subscribing to a pernicious system of exploitation.

According to Krishnamurti's views, Hodson says, the supreme enlightenment of the Lord Buddha is a sham. Nothing of value to Himself or to the world occurred under the Bo-Tree at Buddha Gaya. The whole story has been spread abroad by the Lord Buddha and His disciples as a means of exploiting the people. Krishnamurti would have us believe that the teachings of the Lord Buddha are an imposture. The meaning and purpose of life, the cessation of sorrow, reincarnation, karma, dharma, the noble eightfold Path, arhatship, Adeptship and Buddhahood—all this pure theosophia is poison. The Lord Buddha Himself and every other teacher of these doctrines before and since His advent are poisoners. The Bodhisattva Maitreya, known as the Lord Christ to the West, announced Successor to the Lord Buddha, frankly perpetuates this evil, exists but to despoil humanity of happiness, wisdom, fulfilment. Furthermore, according to Krishnamurti, in Hodson's view, those millions of people who since the founding of Buddhism and throughout the ages have found courage, strength, intellectual and spiritual light and exaltation in the great body of theosophia are all deceived. There is no courage, strength, intellectual and spiritual light and exaltation to be attained as a result of knowledge of the plan of life, the unfoldment of the Divine in Nature and in man and the goal of perfection to which that unfoldment leads. All this is delusion, "a system of thoughtlessness," a net of illusion in which the mind of humanity is hopelessly enmeshed as a result of exploitation by those whom it has regarded as its spiritual superiors.

Such are the logical conclusions to be drawn from the words of Krishnamurti, in Hodson's view. In the people, the motive, says Krishnamurti, is fear, desire for comfort and escape from reality. In their teachers and leaders from the Lord Buddha downwards it is a thirst for power, spiritual ambition and pride.

To those to whom the ideal of discipleship appeals, he says: "You who are seeking satisfaction, what you call happiness, truth, become their tools, and are exploited by these teachers, leaders, and their societies." He also assumes that discipleship means dependence upon a Master by Whom one could be led to Truth, which, of course, never was or could be part of the ideal.

Here it must be admitted, says Hodson, that any listener who, in full awareness has more than once stood in the presence of a Master, who has found himself able to understand, to teach, to enlighten and to heal his fellowmen far more effectively as a result of these experiences than was possible before they came to him—such a person cannot assent to denials of the validity of such experiences in human life. Such denials run counter to a living fact within the listener's own certain knowledge. He knows that as a result of that fact his whole heart opened out more fully in impersonal love for his fellow men, in a more profound compassion and tenderness for all who suffer, for children, the aged, the sick, the downtrodden and the poor. He observes that during the years of his association with the Master, faculties, both of comprehension and of self-expression have been greatly enhanced. He is not deluded into thinking that the Master bestowed these faculties upon him from outside. He knows perfectly well that they were inherent in him from the beginning.

The sun does not bestow upon the plant the power of producing the flower and the seed. Sunshine, however, plays a most important part in the manifestation of that power. Similarly for the disciple, his Master is as a spiritual sun. Indeed, the experience of entering the presence of an Adept is very like that of entering a great light, a centre of spiritual radiance, of power and bliss. Such entrance increases the disciple's own light and power. He experiences his own interior bliss which often is conveyed to others, lightening the burden of their lives and in some cases, not at all rare, reproducing in them the intellectual awakening, the clarity of thought and perception which he himself enjoys.

Those for whom such experiences are a part of the fabric of their existence cannot possibly bring to his teachings that absence of ideas and concepts which Krishnamurti demands from his hearers as an essential to comprehension. It is of no value, it seems to Hodson, to condemn those who from life have wrested certain knowledge: to condemn that knowledge itself as "beliefs" and "self-protective memories, assertions, assumptions." To assert that these are barriers to discernment is to put those who have their own knowledge founded upon direct experience completely beyond the possibility of comprehending Krishnamurti's teachings.

If against this statement it is urged that one does not, cannot know these things direct; that one is depending upon leaders, is self-deceived, and that when the test comes, one's whole scheme of thought will fail one, Hodson says, he can give a personal testimony to the contrary. "I had been a member of the Theosophical Society for two years only when the Great War broke out. I had grasped to some extent the scheme of thought presented in theosophical literature. I knew of the meaning and purpose of life, of reincarnation, *karma,* and the existence within myself of all that is essential to the fulfilment of my life, and had learned that in the acid test I must rely on my own interior life and power alone. For me, as for tens of thousands of my fellow students of theosophy, blind groping had begun to be displaced by intelligent, purposeful living. This was not all book knowledge. Meditation had brought its need of interior realisation. I had discovered and had begun to drink at the inexhaustible well-spring of life within. All this was to be put to severe and prolonged tests. Weeks and months of life under shell-fire, under aerial bombing by night and by day; reconnaissances and actions under fire; long successions of sleepless nights; all these continued until the strain became intolerable. Fear, sheer physical trembling fear, became the ever-present spectre. Friends died by one's side, blown to pieces, burnt to death. Others died of horrible wounds, and others went home shaken and shattered in both body and mind. Throughout all this, Theosophy, especially its affirmation of the immortality and indestructibility of the Self, remained as the one unshakable belief, a rock of ages upon which the mind could and did rest, and resting, drew forth strength and stability which at least prevented outward surrender to fear. During periods of relative rest, meditation on the great theosophical verities never failed to reorient and to re-establish the mind and will upon the centre within. One text from the Bhagavad Gita proved full of power in times of need: it is the great affirmation that: 'He who seeth Me in everything and everything in Me, of him will I never lose hold and he shall never lose hold of Me.'" How can one deny such vital experiences in one's life? What can one say to a teacher who proclaims them superstitions and delusions and brands as exploiters those who affirm them? Hodson queries.

These are questions with which the student of theosophy inevitably finds himself faced when he listens to Krishnamurti, Hodson believes. Either there are logical answers to them or there are not. If there are, they would be most welcome, he says.

3. Exploitation

Having referred to direct experience of theosophical teachings as facts in Nature above, Hodson mentions the experience of discipleship and Krishnamurti's wholesale condemnation of this "most ancient, universal and beautiful ideal." Reasons for condemnation of misapplications of this ideal can readily be seen, Hodson asserts. There are dangers associated with every great adventure, whether material or spiritual. Everest has its ice-walls, crevasses, avalanches, its fierce gales, and its blizzards. Men have perished in attempts to reach the summit. Happily, however, the dangers do not discourage others imbued with the same great spirit of adventure, of sublime aspiration. Indeed, the dangers themselves add to the attractiveness of all great quests. So also is the case of the Everest of the soul, Hodson goes on, the mountain top within. The ascent of man towards great spiritual heights, aspiration to know and learn from Those Mighty Ones who abide upon their summits—this great adventure also has its perils. Here, too, the path leads "twixt cliffs of ice and iron" as every determined aspirant soon discovers. Since Krishnamurti so strongly discountenances the whole idea of the Way of Holiness, the Path of Discipleship and Initiation, Hodson suggests that we look at some of the perils which beset the Soul who seeks to tread that path.

First, it is important to remember that these dangers are not inherent in the path of discipleship itself. They arise from individual perversions of the ideal. Recognition of the possibility of such errors in no way constitutes derogation of one of the noblest ideals by which the mind of man can be inspired. What are the dangers, if any, inherent in the experience of contact with a perfect man? Foremost, perhaps, idolatry; the worship of a perfected personality; its elevation to the position of a god. Against this the Masters have steadfastly warned those who aspire to serve under Them. But it must be admitted that aspirants have been known to fall into this error; one which is readily understandable in view of the enormous evolutionary gulf between the god-like perfection of the Adept and the human limitations of the devotee.

Next of the dangers are pride, self-conceit, the "holier than thou" attitude, Hodson enumerates. Next, the warping of the growth of the Soul. The power of the Adept is said to be so great, His light so dazzling that there may be a danger that the Soul should lose its own individual integrity and become a slavish imitation of that which seems to it so noble, so high. If I understand him aright, Hodson says, this is Krishnamurti's chief objection to the concept of discipleship. He would seem to suggest that, instead of growing by his own inherent power, according to his own spiritual design and towards his own unique attainment, the individual might attempt slavishly to imitate the Master and so miss the experience of making manifest his own spiritual creativeness and of attaining to his own unique fulfilment.

Personally, whilst recognising the others; indeed, observing signs of them in the followers of Krishnamurti; Hodson expresses his profound doubt in the existence of this last danger, particularly when the teacher is a true Adept. The Sun does not impart to or impose upon the plant its own glory; Such is an impossibility even to the Sun. Sunshine assists the plant in the production of its own unique flower, its own fragrance and its own seed. So also the Master, Who is to the disciple as a spiritual Sun in Whose radiance his powers rapidly unfold.

Even if we grant the existence of all these dangers, they do not justify, Hodson submits, the wholesale condemnation either of the Way of Holiness itself or of the aspiration of the Soul of man to discipleship. Concerning the wisdom, love and compassion of the Master Himself by Whom and in Whom that aspiration is fulfilled, it is indeed difficult to justify the uncompromising denunciations of Krishnamurti. Justice, reason, gratitude and respect all seem to me to be outraged in such a condemnation of those Adepts who at this time still take, and from time immemorial have taken, disciples.

Great World Teachers, such as Lord Buddha and Lord Christ, themselves encouraged men and women to seek the heights to which they had ascended, says Hodson. To aid them, These Great Ones drew men near themselves as disciples. Many others among the company of the Adepts perpetuate this practice. Many great servants of humanity have borne testimony to the priceless value of the experience of entering directly the presence of a perfected man. It would seem reasonable, therefore, Hodson submits, to conclude that despite the dangers, there are inestimable advantages to the individual and to the race in the attainment by man of the stages of soul growth known as discipleship, initiation and adeptship.

It is indeed strange that Krishnamurti, Hodson affirms, who has written books of the greatest wisdom and beauty on this very subject, who has personally led many to the feet of the Masters, should in this later phase of his activities now condemn that which once he so highly praised. It is evident that a most radical psychological change has occurred in him. In that change most probably lies the whole secret of so much that is difficult of comprehension in the later phase of his life and work.

The other reasons which he himself gives for his condemnation of his own earlier ideas and teachings are also difficult to follow, as far as Hodson is concerned. He seems to assume that everyone who seeks the way of discipleship does so through motives of fear, of desire for comfort or escape from reality, for spiritual rewards and for gratification of self conceit. Yet he himself, Hodson says, in common with all other authoritative writers, states in his earlier books upon the subject of the spiritual life that these motives would themselves constitute impassable barriers on the path of discipleship. He, therefore, both denies to every aspirant the spiritual light and a state of purity of heart and accuses each and every one of them, from the first disciple on earth to the most recent, of the stupidity of being moved by motives which would inevitably render their quest abortive. A strong and sweeping accusation indeed.

Krishnamurti even goes farther than this, according to Hodson, very much farther. He constantly uses the word "exploitation" as a kind of philosophic club with which to smite the heads of all those who have ever sought and still seek to help others along the path which leads to the Masters' feet. In this category he presumably includes the Adepts themselves.

Discussing the utter incompatibility of his teachings with those expounded by theosophists, he is reported to have said in Mexico: "You cannot give poison from one side and the remedy from the other; that is to say, give with one hand what I call poison; organisation, discipleship, Masters; and with the other the remedy—the remedy against fear, against lack of understanding and intelligence. On the one hand you say: religions are marvellous, necessary; and authority also is necessary for spiritual growth; you say that it is necessary that you should become disciples of the Masters. And then you turn and speak of Krishnamurti who is opposed to all that. One thing is a poison and the other is something that is real; I do not wish that the two things should be mixed."

Apart from the declaration that Theosophy, Masterhood and the Masters are poison and by inference all active theosophists from the remotest ages to the present day are poisoners, one might well enquire for his basis for the words "authority also is necessary for spiritual growth." During twenty-seven years of membership of The Theosophical Society I have heard only the contrary. Man reaches fulfilment by virtue of the release of the life and light within him; this is what I have learned during a prolonged study of theosophy and long association with theosophists. If we are to take Krishnamurti literally, says Hodson, all great spiritual leaders from the beginning of the world, all saints and holy men, all teachers of the Ancient Wisdom, all who have given and still give their lives for the helping of humanity, are exploiters of the people. He will not grant them one virtue. He calls their teachings poison, and their principles pernicious. By assumption, all spiritual teachers, who have appeared in the world up to now, are rogues and self-seeking hypocrites, whilst he alone among them is pure. An astounding phenomenon, indeed!, Hodson concludes.

What is the student to think in the face of such an amazing situation as this? Hodson queries and replies: "I do not answer. I invite answers. I seek understanding; but in the seeking very definitely I am not going to cast away the highest, the holiest, the most beautiful experiences of life. I cannot turn my back upon the great teachers, ancient and modern, who have shed their light upon the world. To do so would be both grave discourtesy and base ingratitude. Since, however, I have so long admired and respected Krishnamurti, I give serious attention to his accusations. Particularly do I give attention to his use of the word 'exploiters' in connection with such people as Madame Blavatsky, Colonel Olcott, Dr. Besant, C. W. Leadbeater and their successors. I have looked at these people with unbiased eyes. I have watched closely for any signs whatever of self-seeking and 'exploitation' in the conduct of their lives and in their relations with their fellowmen, especially with those who have felt most intimately drawn to them. Dispassionately and with every opportunity of knowing the facts, with Krishnamurti's arraignment before me, I have presumed to judge the Theosophical Society, its founders, its leaders and all those tens of thousands who love and serve under them. I give my verdict unhesitatingly. It is: 'Not Guilty.' I believe that these people are working for one object only—to bring to the world the realisation of the fact of the Brotherhood of Man and the other sublime teachings of the Ancient Wisdom. Furthermore, I affirm that in spite of the difficulties which certain of Krishnamurti's teachings create, in spite of the vituperative attacks of one who has been much beloved by them, they are succeeding."

A study of modern thought, scientific, philosophic and spiritual, demonstrates unmistakably that the sixty-four years of work of the Theosophical Society in promulgating these truths is bearing fruit, in Hodson's view. Happily the mind of modern man is gradually—all too gradually, but quite definitely becoming theosophised. And in this lies the hope and the safety of the world in the face of the threat of cataclysmic war. Historians of the future will, Hodson feels sure, see in this relatively small society a movement of immense significance for the whole of humanity. Further he affirms that anyone who denies this can only do so because they have neither realised the true work of the Theosophical Society nor gained any due comprehension through study of the sublime teachings of Theosophy.

4. Incomprehensibility

Hodson proceeds to refer to what he considers another exceedingly strange phenomenon observable throughout Krishnamurti's work. This consists of the confusion of thought into which he throws so many of those who listen to him. Question after question shows that after seven years or more people are still unable to grasp either what he is trying to say or in what way his teachings may be practically applied to life. A significant phrase occurs in the "Newsletter," of March, 1937, says Hodson and quotes: "after the many discussions a certain sense of their futility became apparent." Here is a typical question illustrative of the sense of futility produced in Krishnamurti's listeners: "If we are not to have ideals, if we must be rid of the desire to improve ourselves, to serve God and our less fortunate fellow-beings, what, then, is the purpose of living? Why not just die and be done with it?"

Hodson does not quote the whole of the reply, but a part. "What I have said concerning ideals is this: that they become a convenient means of escape from the conflict of life, and thus they prevent the comprehension of oneself." Is there not something cruelly cynical in thus turning to disrepute the very highest attributes and aspirations of which man is capable by branding them as "convenient means of escape" and by imputation branding all idealists as cowards? Hodson queries. According to Krishnamurti, philanthropy, purity of motive and courage are unknown in the world, especially amongst idealists. Hodson cites another typical question: "I have listened to your talks for several years, but to be frank, I have not yet grasped what you are trying to convey. Your words have always seemed vague to me, whereas the writings of H.P.B., Rudolph Steiner, Annie Besant and a few others have greatly helped me...."

One explanation of this phenomenon offered by his followers, according to Hodson, is that Krishnamurti's incomprehensibility is a sign of his greatness; that if his teachings were easy to understand they would be without value. Hodson'd reply to this would scarcely be polite. He can, however, he says, testify that every great teacher that has preceded him has succeeded in awakening human intuition and enlightened human minds by clear and simple phrases, many of which have come down to us as models of clarity of thought, as utterances pregnant with wisdom. Where abstruse ideas and profound occult and philosophic verities are taught, meditation and close study enable the student to grasp them. Personally, says Hodson, "though I have consulted many, I have yet to meet anyone who can tell me, in a comprehensive way, the general purport of Krishnamurti's teaching. In the main, people seem to be in the same position, either as that so frankly avowed by the questioners quoted above, or as the friend referred to earlier. Personally, I do not for a moment deny or forget that Krishnamurti has given us certain very lofty ideas, nor do I wish here to give the impression that because teaching is difficult it is therefore not exalted."

Indeed, Hodson confesses that he is fully aware that comprehension of great spiritual truths demands a certain stillness of the analytical mind and an alertness of the intuition. Many times, by the very process of trying to listen by intuition, however imperfectly developed, Hodson says he has himself received unforgettable flashes of illumination from Krishnamurti. Indeed, he feels that we should endeavour thus to listen to him. For occasionally there shines out an illuminating truth, a thought, sharp and keen as a sword. Hodson claims, however, that in latter years these occasions appear to have become rarer. One last question may be quoted, he says which would seem to support the possibility that Krishnamurti is becoming less comprehensible as his mission proceeds: "Last Sunday you seemed very uncertain in what you said, and some of us could make nothing of it. Several of my friends say that they are not coming any more to hear you, because you are becoming vague and undecided about your own ideas. Is this impression due to lack of understanding in us, or are you not as sure of yourself as you used to be?"

The answer to this question consists of partial admission of inability precisely to express his ideas in words. According to Krishnamurti's habitual custom, it also throws the onus upon the questioner, suggesting that the blame for the lack of comprehension is largely his own. As I have said, Krishnamurti blames their impurity of "mind-heart," their desire for escape, superstition and beliefs, for his hearers' inability to comprehend him. Is it possible that Krishnamurti is so great that no one can understand him? Can it be that his ideas are so lofty that he cannot put them into words? Is it also possible that his illumination is so transcendental that no one who is not similarly illumined can share in it? Is it that both he and his ideas are so far ahead of the times that the human mind in its present state cannot hope to gain very much from his teachings? Is he speaking to future generations who will perceive and acclaim that to which we of this age are so strangely blind? Is he a spiritual Einstein addressing a humanity still in the kindergarten Hodson queries. And goes on to add that certain phrases and mental attitudes of his would seem to give ground for such a possibility. He himself has said that if three people out of the whole of humanity could understand him he would be satisfied. Whether this minute proportion, this smallness of his hopes is due to the exalted nature of his teachings or the stupidity of mankind, we are not informed, says Hodson.

Against one error Hodson would strongly warn all who listen to Krishnamurti—the error of the dog in Aesop's Fable: He let the substance fall in the hope of grasping the shadow. "During the seven or more years of Krishnamurti's later mission I have seen many promising lives rendered tragically fruitless, many hopes destroyed, and many good servants of humanity lost to that service," Hodson asserts. "Under Krishnamurti's influence they have thrown overboard the whole of life's experiences, life's illuminations, and life's understanding, religion, philosophy, ethics, and even morals—on all these they have turned a scornful back. They have done this in the utterly vain belief that by so doing they will gain some mysterious enlightenment hitherto hidden from them. I have seen noble-hearted, pure-minded men and women, both young and old, throw over their previous moral restraint, cast aside that discipline of life without which there can be no happiness. I have watched them cease from a service to those less fortunate than themselves, which hitherto had made their lives noble and fruitful."

All this they do, as they suppose, at the bidding of

Krishnamurti, says Hodson. "Krishnamurti may be performing one useful function in the world. By his abuse, his denials, his condemnations, he may force us to put our own knowledge again to the test. But when he publicly declares that the Ancient Wisdom is invalid, poisonous, pernicious; when he affirms that he and he alone is showing to the world the way to truth, then I for one must part company with him."

5. Organisations

Krishnamurti is at least consistent in one respect—his general and trenchant condemnation of organisations for the dissemination of doctrines, of societies, orders, ceremonials, says Hodson. This was before the setting up of the Krishnamurti Foundations. The sweeping nature of this condemnation of all organisations for the spreading of spiritual ideas and spiritual life cannot, in Hodson's opinion, be justified. The Solar System itself is such an organisation. The Solar Logos must be regarded both as a great Organiser and as a great Ceremonialist. Just as a wireless receiving set is essential for the receiving of broadcasts or a brain to receive thought, so are world religions essential to the general physical receiving and dissemination of spiritual teachings. Granted, any individual sufficiently advanced, can receive these teachings direct, can, in fact, discover them for himself. The masses, however, cannot as yet do so; hence the need for their guidance of organised methods of teaching. Krishnamurti is himself the centre and the light of an organisation which collects and publishes his authentic teachings concerning self-illumination and the "pathless Reality."

The fact that the organisation itself—or rather its human constituents—tends to become more important than the revealed truths, to be used for the benefit of its officers rather than for humanity, and eventually crystallises the truths and changes them until they are almost unrecognisable—all these evidences of human limitation and error do not do away with the value of such vehicles in the beginning.

Every movement which comes into existence as a vehicle for truth in any aspect does some good, leads some souls to light, serves as a starting place from which some minds set forth on the great search. If only one mind receives illumination the organisation has been worthwhile. For the true illumination of a single mind is of incalculable value to the whole of humanity.

6. Efforts of Comprehension

An intense and prolonged effort of the mind to get behind the words of Krishnamurti, to arrive somewhere, produces strange mental sensations, Hodson comments. "I confess that, apart from rare moments of illumination for which I am profoundly grateful, I find myself for the most part in a maze of somewhat resentful hopelessness. Resentful, when individuals whom I respect and love are vilified and when proven truths are denied. Hopeless, when long-continued study fails to elucidate the teachings. On occasion, however, one has the impression of moving in a very rare atmosphere, a sort of summit-of-Everest consciousness. The very altitude makes everything seem elusive, intangible. Understanding seems near sometimes. One listens or reads on expectant, hoping for the resolution, for the emergent formula or synthesis; but, alas! it seldom, if ever, comes. It is lost—at least for me—in general and sweeping denunciations of some very beautiful things in life, of basic and educative experiences of my own. Premises are thus often unacceptable and this vitiates the conclusions. Always expectant, always hoping, one so often experiences not illumination, but profound disappointment. This may be one's own fault. By his condemnatory attitude to all other spiritual and philosophic teachings than his own, Krishnamurti leads one to expect something utterly different, something unique and new. He seems always to be promising a great illumination, and this it is which produces the heightened sense of expectancy. When after days of listening or hours of reading—every allowance being made for the stupidity with which he charges those who cannot understand him—nothing happens, disappointment becomes inevitable. The mind falls away from the sustained effort to understand that which for it proves incomprehensible. Such are the psychological processes which Krishnamurti induces in me. He will say, no doubt, that this is my fault, not his; that my mind is cluttered up with beliefs, ideals and ideas which completely prevent me from using it intelligently. I have examined this postulated charge, and find that there are four conditions which I demand before I can listen receptively to an exposition of anyone's ideas. These are—First: That people whom I love and revere shall not be unjustly vilified. Second: Reason and logic must not be outraged by self-contradictions and arguments based on premises which are patently unsound. Third: The fact and the value of basic interior experiences, intellectual and spiritual, must not be denied to me. Fourth: I must be permitted to challenge and seek logical bases for dogmatic utterances.

"Surely these four conditions are not unfair. Yet whether listening to or reading Krishnamurti or discussing his teachings with those who proclaim them as a new light, these conditions are never met. In consequence, I find that one Beethoven Symphony, for example, does more for me in an hour than my seven years of study of Krishnamurti's later teachings have done. One great difficulty is that words are not used as men ordinarily use them. Furthermore, affirmations are constantly made which contradict proven knowledge; seem to display both prejudice and ignorance. The presence of personal bitterness shakes one's confidence in the value of the illumination which Krishnamurti claims for himself. All this has been going on for some fourteen years, and we are still no nearer to comprehension. It almost seems a pity that Krishnamurti began his later mission by first denying the validity of the accumulated wisdom of the ages; and, second, by implying that he had discovered and was going to give to the world the only true light. For it is this which produces expectancy of revolutionary teachings and causes the consequent disillusionment when so little emerges."

Even so, he declares, "I am prepared to go on trying. For I have found that by resisting the tendency mentally to leap up and deny, one does sometimes come very near to grasping something of value. Here is an example of an utterance which, whilst almost comprehensible, nevertheless eludes sharply defined apprehension. If it rang true through and through it would solve every problem both of the individual and the race. It may be true, but this expression of it somehow fails to convince—at least, with the admitted limitations of my mind. Question: "How can one be free of the primitive reactions of which you speak?" Krishnamurti: "The very desire to be free creates its own limitation. These primitive or ignorant reactions create conflicts, disturbances and sorrow in your life, and by getting rid of them you hope to acquire something else; happiness, bliss, peace, and so on. So you put to me the question: How am I to get rid of these reactions. That is, you want me to give you a method, lay down a system, a discipline, a mode of conduct. If you understand that there is no separate consciousness apart from the 'I' process; that the 'I' is consciousness itself; that ignorance creates its own limitations, and that the 'I' is but the result of its own action, then you will not think in terms of denudation and acquisition. Take, for example, the reaction towards nationalism. If you think about it, you will see that this reaction is ignorant and very harmful, not only to yourself, but to the world. Then you will ask me: 'How is one to get rid of it'?' Now, why do you want to get rid of it? When you perceive why you want to get rid of it, you will then discern how it has come into being—artificially, with its many cruel implications; and when you deeply comprehend it, then there is not a conscious effort to get rid of this ignorant reaction; it disappears of itself. In the same way, if mind-heart is bound by fears, beliefs, which are so dominant, potent, overwhelming that they pervert clear perception, it is no good making great efforts to get rid of them. First you have to be conscious of them; and instead of wanting to get rid of them, find out why they exist. If you try to free yourself from them, you will unconsciously create or accept other and perhaps more subtle fears and beliefs. But when you perceive how they have come into being, through the desire for security, comfort, then that very perception will dissolve them. This requires great alertness of mind-heart. The struggle exists between those established values and the ever changing, indefinite values, between the fixed and the free movement of life, between standards, conventionalities, accumulated memories, and that which has no fixed abode. Instead of trying to pursue the unknown, examine what you have, the known, the established prejudices, limitations. Comprehend their significance; then they disappear like the mists of a morning. When you perceive that what you thought was a snake in the grass is only a rope, you are no longer afraid, there is no longer a struggle, an overcoming. And when, through deep discernment, we perceive that these limitations are self-created, then our attitude towards life is no longer one of conquering, of wanting to be freed through some method or miracle, of seeking comprehension through another. Then we will realise for ourselves that though this process of ignorance appears to have no beginning, it has an end."

He has read this reply many times, Hodson claims, he has indeed pondered upon it for a long time. He finds that its full significance eludes me. The concept of ignorance, for example, is confusing; for that which exists and has no beginning must be eternal. Therefore, it can have no end. Furthermore, ignorance is hardly an entity, a positive power; surely it is a negation. Nevertheless, in this reply, Krishnamurti comes very near to "letting me through." For one perceives in this teaching a resemblance to the inner significance of the account of Christ stilling the tempest. The disciples—every man—did not fight the storm of life and passion. They awoke the sleeping Passenger, symbol of the Divine within every man as will, as wisdom and clear perception. Once "He" was awake, the storm could not continue to exist. In "His" Presence peace reigned. But I expect that Krishnamurti would deny vehemently that this was what he intended to convey! He and his followers—with apologies for the word used occasionally, faute de mieux—would most probably say that a shallow brain and thought biased by all kinds of fears, beliefs, superstitions, ideals and ideas about Masters could never comprehend. Hodson accepts the charge—humbly—and begs for light—but not at the cost of denial either of reason or of what he knows to be true, he concludes.

7. Escape

Prominent amongst the reasons for Krishnamurti's denunciation of ideals, disciplines and lives devoted to the service of great causes, is that they are all means of escape. The existence of pure idealism, sacrificial love and selfless service by these condemnations is denied. This is an example of the excess by which, in Hodson's opinion, Krishnamurti's teaching is so greatly marred. Perceiving the excesses, repelled by them, one is in danger of casting aside the whole body of his ideas. This, he thinks, would be a profound mistake; for even in the extreme statements, one is not infrequently able to perceive more than a germ of truth. Granted, the ideas thus perceived are in no sense new. One has learnt of them in the course of one's theosophical study. Indeed, everything which is comprehensible and rings true in Krishnamurti's utterances is recognisable as part of the Ancient Wisdom. Krishnamurti's denunciations may apply to some people. But very definitely they do not apply to all. The wise student will use them as a touchstone to his own character and conduct, thereby gaining much of self-purification and reorientation. The brand of "means of escape, fear, search, reward" which Krishnamurti appears to place upon all ideals and all idealists, whilst falsely applied, nevertheless can lead the thought to a great truth, in Hodson's opinion.

"One's theosophical studies show one that the true fruits of life's experiences can only be harvested when they are accepted, entered into in their fullness, examined until their full significance is indelibly impressed upon the consciousness. This is, of course, true of both joys and sorrows. But it would seem to be especially true of sorrow. If those in suffering and sorrow would be wise, they would not, as Krishnamurti would seem to say, run away from these experiences. The waters of such sorrow must be allowed to flow over one, even if one is temporarily engulfed. For in the process of acceptance, examination, and even of being temporarily overwhelmed, the true essence of the experience is distilled within the crucible of the heart. This essence is peace born of comprehension, and he who is able to accept all pain, especially mental pain, with understanding will always find his peace. He who runs away will ever find escape impossible, peace unattainable. This truth is most beautifully expressed in Francis Thompson's wonderful poem, "The Hound of Heaven." The word "Hound" in the title may be taken as a verb meaning 'hunt.'

Krishnamurti expresses this most beautifully—at least, Hodson thinks he does—as follows: "When you begin to suffer, do not say, I must get rid of this or that want or cause, but silently observe, without denial or acceptance (I cannot agree to "without acceptance"—G.H.), and out of this choiceless awareness, want, with its fears and illusions, begins to yield place to intelligence. This intelligence is life itself, and is not conditioned by the compulsion of want."

This idea seems to be susceptible of extension beyond the individual who suffers, Hodson comments. There is only one Divine life, and when, intelligently and without morbidity, we unite ourselves with our own suffering, we unite ourselves with the suffering of all. We become one with them, and in so doing find the peace of the Everlasting Arms—or the Divine compassion without and within—into which we sink, and in which, as we then know, the world is forever safe. This is a mystical experience, which comes as the waters of pain and sorrow are allowed to close over one. In the utter loneliness which accompanies this profound experience, nothing external can aid one. In this complete aloneness beneath the waters of sorrow, comes not only the great peace, but the great illumination of one-ness. The illusion of separateness is gone forever afterwards and with it the illusion of death. A self-conscious awareness of immortality is born out of such an experience. Thus we see the value of life's experiences—Krishnamurti's positive denial notwithstanding, Hodson claims.

Theosophy tells Hodson that it is in experience frankly faced, studied, accepted, that light is found. Pain borne without retreat and without reproach either to life and the pain or to its personal agent, if one exists, karma accepted without bitterness, fear or weakness—in this valiant acceptance, free from the slightest trace of despair or rebellion, lies the way of light.

In one of his most beautiful and revealing utterances, Hodson says, Krishnamurti also expresses this as follows — "As you do not wish to change a lovely form, the glow after sunset, the vision of a tree in a field, so also do not obstruct the movement of sorrow. Let it ripen, for in its own process of fulfilment there is comprehension. When you are aware of the wound of sorrow, without acceptance, resignation or denial, without artificially inviting it, then suffering awakens the flame of creative intelligence."

There speaks the poet, the seer, the illumined, Hodson offers. In such phrases of pure beauty and deep wisdom, Krishnamurti places all lovers of beauty and of truth heavily in his debt. Here we see how true in one sense is Krishnamurti's affirmation that all men, irrespective of evolutionary stature, could enter by this way into this light. Nothing objective bars the way. This liberation is truly available to all. The difficulty is—and we had better face it—that all men are not able to accept suffering without an attempt to evade it and without bitterness or reproach. For such an acceptance demands a certain level of development, a certain almost exalted mental attitude. And to this the average man cannot attain. Furthermore, it is folly, Hodson submits, either to expect him to do so or to condemn him for not doing so. If you do, you break him. His memory drives him instinctively to seek escape from all that is unpleasant; for he thinks that self-preservation lies that way. Yet both his instinct and his thought are wrong. He needs to be instructed in the meaning, cause and cure of pain. This—says Krishnamurti—is where Theosophy is of so great a value to humanity. For this—the meaning and purpose of life and all of life's experience—is part of its great message to the world.

All this would seem to be contained in the story of the Baptism of our Lord, in which He voluntarily entered and was submerged in the waters of Jordan—symbol of the sorrows of humanity, Hodson comments. "He came forth illumined and empowered, as indeed do all who thus receive and welcome the experiences of life. Such, according to theosophy, is part of the great secret of the cessation of sorrow. Krishnamurti undoubtedly does at least hint at this secret which in its essence is less a teaching or description than a vivid experience. For the truth is only fully comprehensible to those who have passed through the experiences. Largely by virtue of one's own experience of life, one is on occasion able to receive from Krishnamurti flashes of illumination, to assent to an idea almost with wonder, so great is the light. Sometimes, however rarely, with a thrill of enlightenment one finds arising from the depths of one's own experience an inner spontaneous answer to his words, Hodson confesses. But—and here is the special warning I venture to give to all who study him, including myself—because he proves illuminating on occasion, do not let us throw overboard all the happiness, beauty and usefulness which our own religion and philosophy have hitherto brought to us. To do so is the wildest folly, and can lead only to sterility, misery, a darkened life."

Questions put to him demonstrate very clearly that Krishnamurti has led people into this darkness, Hodson repeatedly asserts. "I speak feelingly, for I have seen and known so many who have made just that mistake. Once radiant, they are now in darkness. Once loving friends to all, they, like Krishnamurti himself, are now scornful and bitter opponents of their old friends and co-workers. Once useful citizens, they are now idle. Not only are they idle, but they scorn those who remain active in the service of city, country and race. Once self-controlled, vegetarian, teetotallers and refined of speech, they now scorn all systematic discipline, eat meat, smoke, take alcohol and are addicted to coarse language. All this is justified by the plea of fuller self-expression. Great is the tragedy of such temporarily ruined lives—a tragedy all too common since Krishnamurti took up his mission."

Are we to estimate him by such fruits of his teaching alone? Hodson queries. Not entirely, he submits. There is, however, a test which suffices, and for him is final. That test is the extent to which the teacher displays and evokes the quality of compassion. True illumination, he claims, draws the seer nearer to the world, nearer to his brother man and draws his brother man nearer to him. The fact of the oneness of life becomes a living experience. From that experience spring divine love and divine compassion, and at the risk of sounding sentimental, he adds divine sweetness. Wisdom, be it ever remembered, "mightily and sweetly ordereth all things." The true teacher comes "not to destroy, but to build," as some fourteen years ago, and apparently with prescience and purpose, we were all forewarned, Hodson says. To the extent that Krishnamurti or any other both displays and evokes compassion and in the measure in which he "builds," in that measure is he a great teacher. Since Krishnamurti publicly parted company with the Theosophical Society, Hodson affirms, iconoclasm has been a marked characteristic of his utterances. Is it possible that his life is divided into seven-year cycles, each with its own keynote? If so, a new cycle is now opening. Who knows what it may bring? Hodson queries, writing just seven years after Krishnamurti parted ways with the Theosophical Society. No doubt he would have been disappointed in his immediate hopes but his later writings indicate that his views of Krishnamurti grew progressively milder.

A leading Dutch theosophist, J. J. van der Leeuw, analysed some questions brought to the fore by Krishnamurti's critique of Theosophy at a lecture delivered to the London Federation of the Theosophical Society on June 15, to the Dutch Convention on June 21, and to the Geneva Congress of the European Federation on June 30, 1930.

"There was a time when no doubt seemed possible about the future of the T.S.," van der Leeuw begins. "We had been told that the Masters of the Wisdom had founded it and that it was to be the keystone of the religions of the future. Consequently the possibility of its failure hardly occurred to members; empires might crumble, churches might cease to be, but the Theosophical Society would continue throughout the ages. Of late, however, very serious doubts have arisen in the minds of many concerning this future. The world at large is no longer as interested in theosophy or the theosophical movement as it was forty years ago. Then the Society was opposed as a dangerous pioneer movement, now it is regarded with indifference and looked upon as a relic of the past rather than a promise of the future. In almost every section there is a serious falling off of book sales showing that the literature which once appealed to the public is no longer desired."

He then goes on to consider more serious issues even than the indifference of the modern world with regard to the movement which is the conflict within it. He does not speak about a conflict between personalities which, according to him, do not matter. The conflict is one between different standpoints, views of life. He defines these as the conflict between revelation and realization. This conflict has been inherent in the theosophical movement from its inception, in his view and has become acute since 1925.

It was then that on the one hand revelation became fantastic and thereby questionable and on the other hand realization was emphasized by Krishnamurti as the way of life. A system of revelation is only possible, he says, when there is one oracle, or channel of revelation, the authority of which is not to be questioned. A plurality of oracles, he claims, is death to revelation. When in 1925 it was announced that the World Teacher would have twelve apostles as before in Palestine and when Krishnamurti himself denied having any apostles or disciples at all it was inevitable that members should begin to ask whether this revelation as well as previous ones was to be trusted or not.

Previously the ceremonial movements had gained their adherents largely because they were announced as a preparation of the work of the coming teacher, the author goes on. In his name and on his authority were they launched forth and those who took part in them felt they were doing the teacher's work. When he began his teaching and denied the value of ceremonial, calling it an obstacle to liberation, there were again many who asked themselves how this contradiction could be explained. Many and ingenious were the explanations put forward, but the fact remained that the faith in revelation had been shaken forever. The consequence of this has been that the work and self-sacrifice of members in so far as these were based on such faith in revelations, has fallen off considerably. In the hearts of many doubt and despair have taken the place of unquestioning belief. The inevitable result is a process of disintegration, in which many of the most serious members leave a movement in which they no longer have confidence, the author claims.

In his lecture the author seeks out the causes of this disintegration and tries to find a cure. He then proceeds to provide some frank criticism which, he says, has always been exceedingly unpopular in the Theosophical Society. In theory our platform is free, he asserts, but in practice one who thinks differently from the rest, though perfectly free to do so, will find no platform to express his thoughts. There has always been fear of any idea that might disturb the harmony among the members. Criticism, however kindly expressed, he says, was immediately branded as "cruel and unjust attacks," as "unbrotherly" and in the last resort as being under the influence of the Dark Powers. It is the mediaeval attitude of mind where the sulphur smell of Satanic activity is detected whenever an opinion is expressed different from its own.

"In criticizing theosophy we must first of all ask: which theosophy?"he says. "Historically the word means the experience of the divine, in distinction to theology which is discussion about God. This experience of the ultimate, of reality, of life, of truth, is beyond all discussion. It exists wherever a man has it and cannot be criticized or denied. Secondly, the word has been used in an early theosophical manifesto as 'the archaic system of esoteric wisdom in the keeping of the brotherhood of adepts.' ...Thirdly, theosophy is taken to mean the system of doctrines put forward in literature or lectures since the beginning of the Theosophical Society. This is what the world at large knows as theosophy. Finally, there is the practice in important centres of theosophical work, where, in the work actually done and in the aims held before people, we can see what is looked upon as valuable. At the moment I am speaking only about these last two forms of theosophy, that is to say, about that which has been presented to the world in books or lectures or can be seen in centres of theosophical work."

The author claims that this theosophy was born in the Victorian Era. The end of the nineteenth century was a period divorced from life. Man had lost the sense of vital relations and had made objective absolutes out of things which have meaning only as living relations. Thus he looked upon the world surrounding him as an objective universe standing opposite him, independent of his consciousness. Actually what we call the world surrounding us, he notes, is the way in which we interpret the reality that affects our consciousness. This interpretation in terms of our consciousness is our world-image which is real only with relation to the consciousness of which it forms part. As long as this relation is recognized, he argues, all is well; life or reality affects man and through him is externalized as a world-image in his consciousness. Man is the focus through which this process takes place, and there is an unimpeded flow of life reality affecting him and, through him, becoming world-image.

When however, man forgets that he is only a focus of reality and feels himself as a separate being, a soul or a spirit, all changes, the author asserts. Instead of recognizing that what he calls the world is his interpretation, in terms of consciousness, of the reality that affects him, he objectivates that world-image and makes it into an absolute, opposite of him: the world of matter. In a similar way he separates himself from that life which creates the world-image in him, he objectivates that too and calls it God or Spirit. Thus he finds himself isolated between two worlds: a world of gross matter outside and a world of subtle spirit within. This duality henceforth rules his life and in practice he has to choose between its two elements. This choice is one between materialism and idealism.

In the 19th century this antithesis was a very real one, the author proceeds, and theosophy, based on that dualism, identified itself with the idealistic world-view as against the materialistic. It fought the materialism of its day and was frankly idealistic or spiritual in its philosophy. It still is; in theosophical doctrine the spiritual world is looked upon as the real world in which man, the higher Self, has his true home. From that world he descends into these lower worlds of matter where through his "lower bodies" he gathers experience. When, through this experience his Self has become perfected, it returns to that world beyond, whence it came. Thus theosophy is a philosophy of the Beyond; its ultimate reality is not this physical world but a world removed from it by several stages, its fulfilment is not in the present but at a future time when perfection shall be reached. Thus, in space and time, it is a philosophy of the Beyond, he claims.

The world has changed considerably since the 19th century, the author argues. The greatest change has been that it has rediscovered life and thereby re-established the vital relations which were lost in a period of dualism. Thus modern man no longer recognizes a duality of spirit and matter or, in scientific terms, force and mass, but sees these two as convertible quantities which appear as one or the other according to the position of the observer. A new outlook on life has been born which is neither idealistic nor materialistic, still less a compromise between the two. We can define it as a new realism in the light of which idealism appears as outworn as materialism. Its reality is not a world or worlds beyond, but the meaning of this world as of any other world, man being as near to reality in the physical world as in any other world in which he might live. Similarly the fulfilment of life is not seen as a far off apotheosis of ultimate perfection but in the realization of life here and now.

Man himself is the open door to reality, the author goes on to assert, he is the focus through which reality becomes world-image and in his own actual experience of the moment he can therefore find the open door to all life. This is no mystic state, no "merging into the absolute," if such a thing were possible; it is a process taking place in the actual common experience of the actual present moment at the actual place where man finds himself. The experience you have at this actual moment at this place is the open door to reality - nothing else. It is in the here and the now that the way of life is to be found.

The men and women of the new age have therefore no time for a dualistic philosophy which preaches an outworn idealism, he surmises. They have no interest in a philosophy of the Beyond. And such, in their eyes, is theosophy. It was born in an age of dualism, it allied itself with one of its two elements, the spiritual, its reality in a world beyond and its perfection at a future date and is in that respect a relic of the past rather than a promise of the future.

Unless its philosophy becomes one of the here and the now, he warns, recognizing that reality or life can only be approached through the actual experience of the moment, and nowhere else, there is no future for it and it will cease to have other than a historical interest.

Another characteristic of the 19th century was its fear of life, he continues. Where man has disconnected himself from life he is afraid of it and seeks a shelter or refuge. He looks for a final certainty, a system which will solve all problems of life so that Life, which he dreads, shall not be able to take him unawares or upset his comfortable existence. A system of philosophy, therefore, which claims to solve the problems of life and to be able to explain all that happens has a very strong appeal for such a man. Theosophy was such a philosophy; it claimed to have an answer to the problems of life, to have solved its riddles, he argues. Even its enemies must acknowledge that theosophists are unequalled in explaining all that happens, however contradictory. With a true virtuosity they perform the mental acrobatics by means of which they can assert or believe one thing and yet find an explanation when the facts of life contradict it. Here the desire for truth is not so great as the desire to make life fit in with a preconceived system, he concludes. Man feels safe only when nothing that happens to him in daily life escapes the system of rational explanation which he has built up. When something happens to him he wants to explain why it happened and what is it "good for" ultimately. Thus he fits it in into his system of thought; he has rationalized the event.

When Krishnamurti began his teaching the difficulty for most theosophists was not so much that they could not understand the teaching as that they could not fit it into their system of thought. The question was not: What does he mean? but: How can this be reconciled with what we have been taught before? Life, however, can never be reconciled to preconceived thoughts, neither can it be rationalized. Life is not an intelligence, therefore it is neither rational nor logical; it has no cause and no purpose, the author believes. The attempt to rationalize the suffering that comes to us in life, to show that we have deserved it, and that it is "good for something" ultimately, is therefore doomed to failure; we cannot tame life in this way, he asserts.

It is curious to see, according to the author, how man dreads the thought of life being beyond explanation. He wants consolation, a drug which will dull his suffering or a soothing sleeping draught which will give him an illusion of bliss. The theosophist had such consolation and such soporifics. No suffering could come to him, but he would soothe his outraged humanity by a rationalizing process in which he proved to himself that the suffering had to come to him, and that it would be good for him. These attempts at explanations, however, blind man to the true meaning of things that happen to him; they tempt his attention away from the event itself, which again is the here and the now, and lead it to some imaginary cause or result. Thus, the meaning of the event which lies in the actual experience escapes him and he is no richer, no wiser for his suffering, he concludes.

In a similar way, theosophy claims to have an explanation of the great problems of life, he proceeds to explain: why the world was created and how, what happens after death, why man lives and what he will become. Here again, the process of rationalizing leads the attention away from the mystery of life which can only be experienced in the present. Life is not a problem to be solved but a mystery to be experienced. It is the consummate ease with which theosophy explained all problems and all events that has ever made true artists and thinkers fight shy of it, he affirms. They know too well that life cannot be contained in any system, and that the purpose of thought is not to explain life but to understand it, by experience.

A system of thought always brings about a state of mental certainty and repose in which there remains only one fear, that of being disturbed by doubt, according to the author. That is why there has been no place for thinkers in the Theosophical Society; a thinker is always a disturbing influence. Theosophy, by claiming to offer a system of thought that would explain life and its problems, has not only scared away thinkers and artists, but has attracted the mediocre mind that seeks intellectual comfort and not truth. This explains why the theosophical movement, in the fifty years of its existence, has been so singularly lacking in creative or original thought; these were excluded automatically, he asserts.

Once again, he goes on, the great change that has taken place in the world has passed by the Theosophical Society completely. Modern man has rediscovered life and has consequently lost faith and interest in any systems of thought claiming to explain life or solve its riddles. He knows but too well that life can only be understood by the realisation that comes through experience, not by any solutions or doctrines. Our modern age has emerged beyond that narrow conscious life which previously was all that man recognized in his speculations. He is now aware of the unconscious without which the conscious remains unintelligible.

He knows that life, not being 'consciousness,' is irrational and neither logical nor just, according to the author. It is therefore vain to look for ethical explanations of its happenings or moral results of the sufferings it inflicts on us. These can neither explain nor justify the events that take place. The meaning of the event can only be approached through the actual experience of it, and all search for shelter, refuge or consolation leads man away from it. Modern man, therefore, has no interest in a system of thought, however ingenious and elaborate, that would allay his fears and offer him a false repose by its attempts at explaining life. He does not want to be protected; he does not seek the warm and drowsy comfort of the fireside, he would rather go out naked and alone into the storm of life than be safe in a shelter that excludes it. He would rather perish in that storm than live in a false security. He does not seek happiness, but life itself, reality. Therefore, a philosophy which offers him the supposed security of explanations and solutions has no appeal to him, it is no longer valid. He who in these modern days claims to have solved the problems of life only succeeds in compromising himself.

If there is to be any future for the Theosophical Society, the author believes, it will have to renounce utterly its claim of having solved the riddles of life and being a repository of truth; instead it will have to unite those who search for truth and for reality whatever these may bring by way of suffering and discomfort. The seeker after truth welcomes disturbance and doubt, he asserts, the very things which were and are feared most by theosophists. In yet another respect does the Theosophical Society breathe the atmosphere of last century. It is in the desire to unite in one brotherhood all who think or feel alike. Thus the Theosophical Society aimed at forming a nucleus of brotherhood. Such a nucleus however always defeats its own ends. It cannot escape becoming a brotherhood with the exclusion of less desirable brethren. The moment we unite a number of people in such a nucleus we have created a sect, a separate group walled off from the rest of the world and thereby from life.

We show the truth of this each time we speak, the author asserts, as we so often do, of the "outside world". The words imply that we ourselves are inside something. Inside what? Inside something that keeps that "outside world" outside that same something! Inside a barrier which we have erected around us and by means of which we have shut out those who think differently. That barrier of elaborate beliefs and doctrines has so efficiently shut out the dreaded "outside world" that no fresh air from that world has succeeded in penetrating its inner fastnesses, and the Society has breathed for fifty years nothing but the atmosphere of its own thoughts and beliefs. At its meetings it was always theosophists who told other theosophists about the theosophical doctrines which they all knew already. The one thing that was prevented unanimously was the introduction of foreign ideas which might challenge or doubt the established doctrines. This exclusion of the outside world has been most manifest in the lodge life. It was in the snug and stuffy intimacy of lodge life that theosophical orthodoxy could breed; there, in a small circle of mediocre minds, all thinking and believing alike, a warm brotherliness could arise, uniting all in the delightful certainty of possessing the esoteric truth while the outside world lived on in darkness.

On his last lecture tour he visited a lodge, the president of which told him that his lodge was "just one happy family," the author discloses. "This roused my misgivings, for I know what such happy families are like. Then he continued saying that a few years back there had been a member who was always questioning and challenging everything, causing disturbance at their otherwise harmonious meetings. But now that member had left their lodge, and all was harmony again. He meant, of course, that the blissful drowsiness of their intellectual slumber which had for a while been disturbed by the one member who happened to be alive had been re-established."

It is quite true that, theoretically, our platform is free, the author admits, that we have no dogmas, and that everyone is free to criticise. But if he does, he will suffer a silent excommunication which will effectually cold-shoulder him out of the nucleus of brotherhood. He will be made to feel that his conduct is scandalous and unbrotherly, that he is in the throes of the lower mind, that he is attacking theosophy, and laying himself open to the influence of the Dark Powers. And this attitude holds good not only among groups of ignorant members; he claims to have found it right up to the highest authorities. Therefore, the talk about a free platform and the perfect freedom of thought does not impress him for he says he knows that there is no such freedom, but rather an unconscious orthodoxy that has almost succeeded in killing out the critical faculty among theosophists altogether. If the Society, in its pride, had not been so certain that it walked in the light and had been called to bring this light to a world in darkness, it might have noticed that the barriers, which it built up between itself and the outside world, prevented the light of life from coming in, so that it lived in darkness, while in the outside world a new and great light had arisen. That world has rediscovered the life about which theosophists talked, and consequently, it will not suffer any more barriers. Therefore truly modern men and women will no longer become members of any society, so long as they feel that its brotherhood is a sect and its freedom of thought an orthodoxy. The "outsider" feels that, by entering the Theosophical Society, or any other spiritual movement, he subscribes to a creed which excludes him from the rest of the world, and enters a brotherhood which will make him different from all who do not belong to it.

If the Theosophical Society is to survive, the author warns, if it is to attract those whom it has always endeavoured, and generally failed, to attract, it will have to change its ways entirely. Above all, the traditional lodge with its traditional meetings should be abolished. There is no more dreadful mutual burden than that of the lodge which has to meet every Tuesday night and then think of something to do. The result must be a burden or an artificial semblance of life.

Once again, he warns, if the Theosophical Society is to continue, the old form of membership which implies the silent acceptance of a creed must go, and a loose organisation take its place in which membership no more makes a man part of a sect than would, for instance, membership of the

National Geographic Society. Modern man will suffer no barriers that shut life out in a supposed "outside world"; he seeks the free and unimpeded contact with life.

II

Having dealt with the causes of the decline of the theosophical movement in its relation to the world at large, he proceeds to consider the more serious causes of disintegration within the movement. From its very beginning the Society has suffered from an internal conflict which he has characterized as that between realization and revelation. In its historical meaning theosophy means realization, the experience of the Divine within man. In that sense, it was used in Neo-Platonic philosophy and by mediaeval philosophers. This conception of theosophy has been present in theosophical teachings from the beginning. A man was to find the higher self within him and thereby come into conscious unity with the Life in all things. At the same time, however, theosophy is characterised as "the archaic system of esoteric truth in the keeping of a brotherhood of adepts." Here theosophy is not a truth to be experienced by man in himself, it is a body of doctrine possessed and guarded by a group of Adepts in whose power it lay to reveal it to others. Thus the way of knowledge became one of discipleship; only by becoming a pupil of one of the Masters could man hope to partake of the esoteric truth. The aim was to gain initiation into the Brotherhood, to enter the hierarchy that guarded the esoteric wisdom. This way of knowledge is one of revelation; the divine Wisdom is received by the pupil from his Master and handed on again by him to those less enlightened than himself. Thus a hierarchic system of revelation arises in which the authority of superiors is not to be questioned and the slightest hint is an order not to be criticised but to be obeyed. The spirit is that of a spiritual army where obedience and efficiency are greater virtues than individual creative activity and genius. The way of realisation is the way of the individual; its highest product is the creative genius. The way of revelation is the way of the group; its highest product is the perfect channel, obediently transmitting orders and power from above.

We must sharply distinguish revelation from authority, the author asserts. Authority is a fact in nature; where a man is superior in wisdom or power he will automatically have authority over others. That this authority can lead to abuse of power or to tyranny and impede the freedom of others does not invalidate the fact that superiority in any respect means authority.

But when the author speaks of revelation, he means all information claiming to come from an unseen source, from an inaccessible authority. Primitive man looked upon some few as being intimately related to the gods he feared and being able to reveal their will and power. Thus the priest was a channel through whom the will, the knowledge and the grace of the deity could be transmitted to the masses. Man sought for guidance of his own life by the revelations coming to him through the appointed oracle. The priesthood thus gained power over man's soul and was able to enforce its own will by clothing it in the garment of revelation from above. Therefore, revelation in the meaning in which the author uses it, is a message from an unseen authority coming through an appointed channel.

In ordinary speech, he says, we sometimes talk of things being "a revelation to us," but that is not the sense in which the word is used by him. He says he can say that the Einstein theory is a revelation to him, but it will be clear that no scientific work ever partakes of the element of revelation. It does not speak in the name of an unseen authority, the scientist speaks in his own name and what he says can be questioned, criticised, proved or disproved. The authority is always available, the source of knowledge is accessible and, even though not every man has the means to prove whether the Einstein theory is true or not, he knows that Einstein's brother scientists have done their utmost to discover a flaw in it.

The bulk of the theosophical literature does not partake of the element of revelation, in the author's view. If a theosophist writes a book describing his experiences in this or other worlds, or expounding his ideas on life and its problems, there is no revelation in such a work. The one who wrote it is available, can be questioned and criticised, the argument of the book can be discussed and contradicted; the entire subject remains within the realm of reason. Yet even in the time of H.P.B. the element of revelation was present in the Theosophical Society. Thus, in the Mahatma Letters we find messages coming from an unseen authority through an appointed channel.

Later on, when letters were no longer forthcoming, messages came directly through certain recognized theosophical authorities, the author maintains. In these messages, the Masters would express their desires as to what should be done or not done, what activities undertaken or opposed, and give hints guiding the lives of prospective pupils. Here we find real revelation: messages from an unseen authority, inaccessible to others. Theoretically, of course, the unseen authority is accessible to all who succeed in raising their consciousness to its level; practically it is not, and should any claim to have come into touch with the same authority from whom messages were previously received through another, that authority usually speaks through him with a very different voice. We only need to compare the letters from the Master K.H. produced in the time of H.P.B. and written in her Bohemian manner interspersed with French expressions, often somewhat racy in style, with the messages revealed as coming from that same Master in recent years. They breathe an utterly different spirit; where the former denied the existence of God in any form, seen or unseen, personal or impersonal, the latter have reintroduced him in a very personal way indeed. Where in the Mahatma Letters the Master K.H. speaks of religion as being the greatest evil in human civilisation, and denounces all churches, priesthoods and ceremonials in definite terms, his more recent messages speak with great reverence about religion and church and endorse ceremonial and priesthood most vigorously. One is therefore inclined to think that the source of unseen authority for each is a strictly individual and subjective one, an exteriorisation of his own unconscious motives. This is still more evident with regard to all messages revealed as coming from the World Teacher during the last fifteen years.

When Krishnamurti began speaking on his own authority, and in his own name as the World Teacher, the things he said were widely different in spirit and purpose from all messages thus received. First of all, he emphatically denied being the vehicle of another consciousness or being used by anyone who spoke through him or inspired him. He claimed to be the World Teacher, not because some other intelligence possessed or used him, but be cause he had gained liberation and become one with life, which is the only Teacher.

Krishnamurti utterly denied having any apostles or even disciples and rejected ceremonials, however and wherever used, as an obstacle on the path to liberation. Neither would he have anything to do with the occult path of discipleship and initiation, characterising all these as "unessentials." It was therefore inevitable that theosophists all over the world should have begun to doubt all previous revelations and to suspect that these were more in the nature of subjective opinions.

It takes the mental acrobatics of trained theosophical students to reconcile the contradictory facts contained in the earlier revelations and the subsequent teaching of Krishnamurti. Even though he himself strongly denies being used by another consciousness, they claim to know better than he does what is actually taking place in his own consciousness, and still maintain that there is another person, the "real" World Teacher, living in the Himalayas, who occasionally speaks through Krishnamurti. This real World Teacher entirely endorses all previous revelations, he has apostles and approves the ceremonial movements, especially the Liberal Catholic Church. The fact that Krishnamurti denies the value of all these is then explained by the fact that he, being "only a vehicle", cannot express fully the "glorious consciousness" which they, the speakers, know so much more intimately than he. Thus it means nothing that he should contradict things previously revealed, it only shows that at that time, it was not the World Teacher speaking — but only Mr. Krishnamurti. The interesting situation arises that a few people are to be credited with the ability to tell us when Krishnamurti speaks and when the World Teacher is speaking.

The result would seem to be that when the opinions agree with their own, it is the World Teacher speaking, while otherwise it is Mr. Krishnamurti. The only one who evidently is not to be believed, when he says the World Teacher is speaking, is Mr. Krishnamurti himself. It is needless to expound further the length to which theosophical casuistry can go; the tragical fact remains that there appears to be less desire to understand what Krishnamurti says than to fit it in with revelations previously given. It would be far simpler to recognize the previous revelations to have been erroneous. But this, of course, would discredit the cause of revelation.

Enough, however, has been said to show how fatal the effects of revelation are in any movement. The fact that revelation is a message coming from an unseen authority, inaccessible to others, places it beyond the realm of reason and makes it impossible to criticise or discuss its value. "In all discussions which I have ever had on the subject the adherents of revelation would always end by saying, 'Well, all I can say is that the Master told me to do this, and so I do it.' This ends any discussion, and puts the question beyond reason. Thus I maintain that the evil effects of revelation are caused by the fact that revelation can only be accepted or denied, but never criticised in the light of reason. I know that theoretically this can be done, and whenever the subject is brought up, we are told that theosophical leaders have always urged their disciples to judge for themselves and not accept anything because they said it. This, however, is theory; in practice, one who ventured to criticise or doubt a message coming from the Master, would suffer the silent excommunication of the heretic, and be made to feel that he was unfit to be of the elect. Of what value is the freedom to criticise and to judge for oneself when, in the rare cases, where some brave soul has ventured to do so, we are told that 'in incarnations to come, he will, through untold suffering, grope in vain for the light which he thus wilfully rejected'? This is but Eternal Damnation in another form. It is the threat and fear of punishment to come which terrorises the would-be critic back into an attitude of obedient submissiveness. In the Mahatma Letters and the correspondence between H.P.B. and Sinnett, we can read what is said about those who do not take a hint once given, or who dare to argue about an order coming from above."

Even Sinnett himself was repeatedly threatened with the breaking off of all further intercourse with his Master if he did not follow the orders given, according to the author. He feels there is no doubt that, if a theosophist at any time criticises or rejects a message coming to him from the Master through an appointed channel, he will thereby be said to have cut himself off for a long time to come from any further such privileges. Where simultaneously discipleship and a drawing nearer to the Master are held up as the goal of life, it is clear that the theoretical freedom of criticism means the giving up of all that is held dearest and highest in the life of theosophists. He wishes to make it perfectly clear that he is in no wise denying the existence of the Masters or the possibility of communion with them. If he thinks that the Master has spoken to him, this fact implies no revelation, but only experience: "I have an experience which may or may not be of value to me." Revelation only begins when he transmits to others the messages thus received as coming from that unseen authority. He suggests that anyone who thinks he or she has received a message or order from a Master or higher authority should first see whether he himself agrees with it, whether it awakens a response in his own soul. If so, let him, when speaking about it to others, speak in his own name and say, "I think this, and I will this". But never let him say, "The Master thinks this or the Master wills this". Should he himself not agree with the communication thus received, let him say nothing at all. But let him never speak in the name of an unseen authority. Revelation is still more fatal when it interferes with the life of the individual and attempts to guide his life, to tell him what to do or where he stands. It has been the custom in theosophical centres to look to a few as being able to tell others where they stand in their spiritual evolution, whether they have taken a step forward or not. Thus spiritual progress is made to depend on revelation, and power is given to a few to tell others where they stand. The consequences of this are always fatal, the author claims. The absurdity of the situation becomes clear when we consider that if these few people, supposed to be able to tell us where we stand, were to die, we should be lost in uncertainty. Again, if the appointed channels should disagree, as has happened before, we have to choose whom we are going to believe and whom not! It is inevitable that where such power is placed in the hands of the few, their own personal likes and dislikes will unconsciously influence the occult standing they confer on others. These, on the other hand, may be afraid to contradict or oppose one who has the power to bestow or withhold steps, but will try to keep in good standing, and do what they are asked to do. Thus a host of spiritual inquiries are born, detrimental to the individual and to the cause he serves. But above all, the fact remains that it is impossible at any time for any one to tell another where he stands in spiritual progress. No one can reveal that to you but the life that is in you. Each individual is as a ray going forth from the centre of the circle; he can only enter the centre of life along the ray that is his own being, never along another. Life expresses itself in each one of us in a way which we alone, and no one else, can know; there is a sanctuary of life in each of us where we alone can enter and hear the voice of. We cannot enter that sanctuary by the backstairs of revelation; there is only the royal road of our own daily experience of life. No one can tell you what to do in life, the author believes, what work to serve but the voice of life that is within you, your own inner vocation, your individual uniqueness.

To go to another, and to ask him what you should do or where you stand is to violate the life that is within you, in the author's opinion, and to shut yourself off from it. He emphasizes that he does not deny the existence of the occult path or the steps on it such as discipleship or initiation. Their existence or non-existence lies outside the subject I am dealing with. The element of revelation only enters where any one, in the name of an unseen and inaccessible authority tells others where they stand and what steps they have taken, so that no one is supposed to have taken a step unless one of the few acknowledged channels of revelation has affirmed him to have done so.

Nothing would be lost if this practice with all its fatal consequences were discontinued. If the taking of a step means an expansion of life within, that expansion will be there and show itself whether anyone else says you have taken a step or not. What would it avail you if everyone acknowledged you as having taken a step and the expansion of life were not within you, and on the other hand, what do you lose if everyone should agree in saying you have not taken a step and the expansion of life is in you and shows forth in your daily life, he queries. The telling or not telling is wholly unessential and wholly mischievous in its consequences. It makes for a spiritual snobbery in which the elect sit in the seats of honour, while the common herd are despised.

Though the results of revelation are always fatal, the author warns, and opposed to the spirit of theosophy, which is realisation, it is most dangerous where it interferes with the individual lives of people and attempts to make them cease from work they are doing or undertake work they have no intention of doing. Especially where young people are concerned such interference is inexcusable. He says he knows cases where, on the basis of revelation, young people have a few been taken out of their university studies in order that they might dedicate themselves to "the Work." As if the Work for each one were not that which the life within him urges him to do, instead of the revelation coming from another! In modern education, especially in the Montessori method, it is fully recognized that the way of life is the way of realization. The child is surrounded by didactic material, the only purpose of which is to draw out its faculties and to enable it to learn by experience. In this way the child will spontaneously grow into that which the life within it means it to be.

Opposed to this spirit of life, according to the author, is the army spirit where orders come from above and have to be obeyed without argument or delay. It is this spirit which inevitably accompanies revelation; a spiritual hierarchy is like a spiritual army where orders are obeyed and not questioned. In this army-spirit individual uniqueness and creative genius are crushed out. We cannot therefore wonder why there has been so little creative work in the Theosophical Society; it is because the ideal of the "band of servers" has been obedience to revelation, and not self-expression through realization. There is no reason why anyone should not occasionally seek the advice of those wiser than himself, and discuss with them his difficulties. There is no reason why we should not try to learn as much as we can from teachers and books, so long as we realize that we have to make our decisions in our own name and that it is weakness to shift the responsibility on to others.

We must have no fear to guide our own lives, he believes. Better to perish in the attempt than go safely along the way of another. There is no future for the Theosophical Society unless the evil of revelation be shaken off, never to return. It is wholly incompatible with theosophy which is essentially experience of the Divine, or realization. It is not another "path" or "aspect"; superstition is no path, but an error. There is a pseudo-tolerance which agrees with the most conflicting views, admiring them all impartially, and trying to get "some good out of each one." This tolerance is in reality a lack of backbone, an absence of vigorous life.

"Let no one say that in my address I have denied occultism. There is a future for occultism if it will conform to strictly scientific methods, and submit to tests and proof. It can only develop if it renounces entirely all spiritual or religious claims; it has as little to do with these as ordinary science. Just as science could not develop until it shook off the mystical and spiritual glamour with which it was enveloped in the Middle Ages, so the condition of progress for occultism as a science is that it should likewise discard the halo of mystery in which it is enveloped."

When the question is asked: Has the Theosophical Society a future, the author says he can only answer that he does not know. But what he says with utter certainty is that it has no future unless it breaks free from the outworn mentality that still permeates it and is born anew in the spirit of the new age. That spirit is one of love of life instead of fear of life, one in which life is welcomed even though it may destroy the beliefs in which we found refuge hitherto. Theosophy must cease to be a philosophy of the Beyond; it must conquer the duality in which it is still rooted and realize that the open door to reality lies in the here and the now, in man's actual daily experience and not in some higher world or some distant future. None can open this door for us and none can close it. It is no mystical experience for the few alone; it is for all and it is only our fear of life that makes us incapable of seeing it.

Theosophy, the author insists, has to realise that its claim of being a philosophical system, explaining the problems of life, has no appeal to modern man who knows that life is not a problem to be solved; to whom it is a search and an ever - increasing experience. The Society must cease to be a brotherhood with the exclusion of less desirable brethren; it must break down the barriers which make it possible to speak of an "outside world", and create a new form of membership which does not involve sectarian allegiance. Above all, theosophists must learn to recognize the conflict that has been inherent in theosophy from the beginning: that between realization and revelation. Theosophy, as the realization of life by each man in his own consciousness, is incompatible with a hierarchic system of revelation where truth and enlightenment come to us through others and where the guidance of our life rests on orders received from superiors. Modern man no longer desires a shelter or a refuge, consolation or security. Rather than stagnate in the false repose and happiness which these can give, he will go out alone and face the storm of life on his own strength. The aim of theosophy is to breed, not weaklings, but strong men, he concludes.

Perhaps the most comprehensive assessment of Krishnamurti from the theosophical point of view is the study *Krishnamurti and the World Teacher Project* by Govert Schuller.

The author, Govert Schuller, was born and raised in the Netherlands. He first came in contact with Theosophical teaching while still in high school through a Theosophical friend. Mr. Schuller studied philosophy for three years at the Universities of Leyden and Amsterdam. He emigrated to the United States with his wife in 1990 and is currently doing research on Krishnamurti. He and his wife now live in Carol Stream, Illinois, which is near the headquarters of the Theosophical Society in America.

In his introduction, Schuller says that the centennial of Krishnamurti's birth gave him the idea to present an overview of the different ways he has been perceived in the

Theosophical movement. As there is such a wide variety of Theosophical ideas about the person Krishnamurti and his teachings, he limited the scope of his analysis to the perceptions of Krishnamurti, which primarily concern themselves with the metaphysical status of Krishnamurti as a spiritual teacher. Those views primarily concerned with the metaphysical importance of his teachings are left out. It is inevitable, though, he feels, to include some quotes dealing with the content of his teachings to clarify the views about Krishnamurti. Having limited the field of inquiry, he advances the thesis that the vast majority of these views can be differentiated according to a matrix determined by the way Theosophists answered two basic questions concerning Krishnamurti.

The first question concerns the expectation of and preparation for the coming of a great spiritual teacher as was announced by Annie Besant, then President of the Theosophical Society. Schuller cites a lecture at Madras on December 31, 1909, in which she made the statement that a great "Teacher and Guide....will deign once more to tread our mortal ways." Together with her colleague and friend Charles W. Leadbeater, Besant propagated the idea that young Jiddu Krishnamurti would be the vehicle through whom this teacher, the Christ or the Lord Maitreya, would manifest, as he had done two thousand years earlier when he had worked through Jesus of Nazareth during his ministry in Galilee. They then founded the Order of the Star in the East, with Krishnamurti as its head, in order to bring together those who believed in the coming of this teacher. The important question for many Theosophists at the time, according to Schuller, was, and for some still is: Was this project genuine or not? The term genuine does not necessarily refer to the correctness of how Annie Besant and C.W. Leadbeater perceived and propagated this project, but it refers to whether the project was perceived as having its origin in a transcendental source of supreme intelligence regardless of how it was interpreted by human agents.

The second question was and is perceived by Theosophists as even more important, according to the author. It concerns the result of this project: Was the outcome of the project successful or not? Here again the term successful does not necessarily refer to the way in which the project was expected to be successful, but rather to the fact that the outcome of the project was perceived as having fulfilled the original intention of the transcendental source of intelligence. The point of this nuance about the meaning of the concepts "genuineness" and "success" is to be able to include viewpoints which do not exactly corroborate, but are close to Besant's and Leadbeater's statements about the project.

The possible answers to these two questions generate the four following positions:

1) The project was perceived as genuine and successful;
2) The project was perceived as genuine, but failed;
3) The project was perceived as not genuine and failed (of course); and
4) The project was perceived as not genuine, but succeeded!

The theosophical commentators and ideas presented by the author are classified accordingly. This treatment is not exhaustive, he admits, since many views are excluded. The criteria of selection are: importance of the source, in the sense that the person propagating the view is regarded as important as an independent teacher of theosophical ideas; originality of the view, in the sense that the view helps to open up the complexity and multi-dimensionality of the whole issue; and accessibility of primary sources to avoid erroneous hearsay. In some cases, the author includes Krishnamurti's own reply to the views put forward.

As position two is taken by many persons, the author argues, it is inevitable to give that relatively more space, as is inversely the case with position four. The view of each person discussed is presented as much as possible in his or her own words. In the cases where a "Master of Wisdom" or "Adept" is quoted, nothing definite is implied about his ontological status or the veracity of his statements. Krishnamurti's view of himself is included in this discussion. His view can be seen as belonging to position one, according to the author.

The study closes with four additional views of Krishnamurti, which, according to the author, are all important from an epistemological perspective. The first two, he says, are not rooted in a theosophical world view but are based on direct observations of Krishnamurti and as such not classifiable in the proposed matrix. They are important, however, because any future theosophical theory about the metaphysical status of Krishnamurti will have to take these observations into account. They provide building-blocks, yet uncoloured by theosophical concepts, to be incorporated in a theosophical or psychological theory. The third view is theosophical and is important because it makes a beginning with putting the two non-theosophical views in a theosophical perspective, though not in such a way as to be classifiable according to the matrix. In fact it takes an interesting epistemological meta-position about the matrix in its entirety, according to Schuller, as does the last view. These last two views belong to a classification, which encompasses at least three different epistemological attitudes towards metaphysical knowledge. 1) theosophical: One has access to and knowledge about the metaphysical realm of noumena. Intuition, deep speculative reasoning, clairvoyance and revelation provide us with that access. 2) Agnostic: One acknowledges the possibility of access to and knowledge about the metaphysical realm, but does not have it (yet). 3) Kantian: One can not have access to and knowledge about the metaphysical realm. Knowledge can be attained only about phenomena, not about noumena.

Having stated the various positions regarding the World Teacher Project, however, Schuller does not proffer any final judgement on which he considers to be the more credible proposition, such a judgement being beyond the purview of a historian in his view.

Accessing Krishnamurti's Insights

However history may judge Krishnamurti, ultimately the impact he makes on posterity will depend on how it is able to access and benefit from his insights. Several attempts have been made to do so. The reader is the best judge of their effectiveness. Neurolinguistic Programming (NLP) is one of the tools used for this purpose. NLP is an ensemble of ideas designed to model excellence in every field. A basic idea of what it comprises and how it can be used to access Krishnamurti's insights is given below.

The scene is a seminar for businessmen, managers, executives, professionals and health care personnel. The man conducting it is Richard Bandler, a mathematician and co-founder (with John Grinder, a computer expert) of a discipline they term neuro-linguistic programming (NLP).

Bandler tells his rapt audience: "I'd like you to try some very simple experiments, to teach you a little bit about how you can learn to run your own brain. Think of a past experience that was very pleasant—perhaps one that you haven't thought about in a long time. Pause for a moment to go to that memory, and be sure that you see what you saw as that pleasant event happened. You can close your eyes if that makes it easier to do...

"As you look at that pleasant memory, I want you to change the brightness of the image, and notice how your feelings change in response. First make it brighter and brighter... Now make it dimmer and dimmer... Now make it brighter again. How does that change the way you feel? There are always exceptions, but for most of you, when you make the picture brighter, your feelings will become stronger... And decreasing the brightness usually decreases the intensity of feelings.

"How many of you ever thought of intentionally varying the brightness of an internal image in order to feel different? Most of you just let your brain randomly show you any picture it wants, and you feel good or bad in response. Now think of an unpleasant memory, something you think about that makes you feel bad. Now make that picture dimmer and dimmer... If you turn the brightness down far enough it won't bother you any more...Brightness is one of the many things you can vary—others are size, colour, distance, depth, duration, clarity, contrast, slide or movie, speed, transparency, etc. For those of you who really want to learn to run your own brain, take any experience and try changing each one of these visual elements."

Bandler goes on to disclose other techniques to tackle the participants' embarrassing experiences in their past: run a mental movie of such an experience and if it still makes you feel bad, run it again but this time playing circus music as you do so! Alternatively run the movie backwards from finish to start as if you were rewinding it, very fast. Bandler guarantees that tragedies can be turned into comedies in this way.

Although NLP was unveiled by its founders over a decade and half ago it took time to gain popularity partly because of its intimidating title. However, it has since been gaining momentum thanks to popularisers like Anthony Robbins (*Unlimited Power*) and Dr Harry Alder (NLP—*The New Art and Science of Getting What You Want*) who have written bestselling books on the subject. Bandler's and Grinder's own books were privately published and did not gain a wide audience.

NLP practitioners have begun to discover a wide repertoire of psychological techniques to improve their abilities and behaviour.

For example, those who need to, but have difficulty in

seeing a situation from anyone else's point of view can try this prescription: First run a movie of the event in question in your mind as you remember it; then run a movie of the same event , looking at it over the other person's shoulder so you can see yourself as the argument takes place. Go through the same movie from the beginning to end , watching from this viewpoint. It can make a huge difference, according to Bandler.

An important concept in NLP is of associated and dissociated memories. "Associated means going back and reliving the experience seeing it from your own eyes...You may see your hands in front of you but you can't see your face...Dissociated means looking at the memory from any point of view other than from your own eyes... as if you were someone else watching a movie of yourself....When you recall a memory associated you re-experience the original feeling response that you had at that time. When you recall a memory dissociated you can see yourself having those original feelings in the picture, but without feeling them in your body...The ideal situation is to recall your pleasant memories associated, so that you can easily enjoy all the positive feelings that go with them. When you are dissociated from your unpleasant feelings you will still have all the visual information about what you may need to avoid or deal with in future, but without the unpleasant feeling response. Why feel bad again?... What you are teaching your brain to do is to associate with pleasant memories and dissociate from unpleasant ones. Pretty soon your brain will get the idea and do the same thing automatically with all your other memories." Bandler emphasises that "teaching someone how, and when to associate or dissociate is one of the most profound and pervasive ways to change the quality of a person's experience, and the behaviour that results from it."

An extreme form of unpleasant experience with permanent effect is a phobia, that is, fear of dogs, spiders, flying, lifts ... NLP teaches you to get rid of phobias instantly. Try this prescription: First imagine you are sitting somewhere in the middle of a movie auditorium. On the screen project a black and white photo of yourself just before you acquired your fear of it. Next, leaving your body in the auditorium, position yourself in the projection room from where you can see yourself watching your photo on the screen. Now transform that photo on the screen into a black and white movie and watch it from the beginning to just beyond the end of the critical experience. Now turn it again into a slide, jump into the picture and run the movie backwards, but when you run it backwards make it a colour movie and run it so fast it is rewound in a couple of seconds. The exercise should get rid of your terror. Bandler has observed that people who are terrified of even mentally witnessing an unpleasant scene do not mind watching themselves witnessing the incident, and has used NLP to exploit the situation.

People who lack motivation can benefit greatly from NLP. They should find a friend who has high motivation and question him how he runs the movies in his mind to motivate himself. Most of us may not be aware of what we are doing to persuade ourselves to get up early in the morning, for example, and set out for work. By questioning motivated friends closely what images arise first in their minds that prompt them to jump out of bed, you can do likewise. For instance, a regular early riser may see a bright image of himself doing something he enjoys doing. That motivates him to get up early and forget his physical discomfort. The same process will probably motivate him in whatever else he does.

Most of us suffer from limiting beliefs of all kinds. We may believe that we are unable to drive in crowded roads, that we lack organisational ability, that we lack the will power to lose excess weight, that we will be unable to learn to swim or be an expert tennis player, and so on. Here is the NLP procedure to eliminate that crippling belief that stands in the way of your success: First find out how you represent mentally your limiting belief. Let's say you believe you lack the will-power to lose weight. How do you represent it in your mind? Do you see yourself as fat in bright colours? Or is the image blurred? What is the size of the picture? Is it three dimensional or two dimensional? Take some time to experiment and find out. Next, think of how you represent doubt internally, that is, something which you may feel may or may not be true. For example, you may have doubts about your ability as a tennis player. Or you may have doubts about the efficacy of some medicine. What is the difference in terms of size of picture and other characteristics discussed earlier? One by one test each characteristic for its ability to change your belief into doubt. That is, change the characteristics of how you picture yourself losing weight into the characteristics of how you picture yourself playing tennis or how you picture the doubtful efficacy of the medicine in question.

After testing each characteristic change back to the old one before testing the next characteristic. What new belief would you like to substitute for the earlier limiting one? State it positively: 'I can easily lose weight.' While maintaining the internal representation of your limiting belief, change all the characteristics to those which express doubt most powerfully, for example if belief is represented by a movie and doubt by a still picture, freeze the movie. Then change the content to express the new belief you wish to install and finally change the characteristics of doubt to those of belief. For example, you surely believe that the sun will rise tomorrow. How to you visualise this belief? Note down each characteristic. Change the characteristics of the picture of yourself losing weight, after you have altered them to the characteristics of yourself playing tennis—then change them into the characteristics of your belief in sunrise. That should do the trick.

Most of us would like to be able to give up some of our habits, (defined as an automatic response over which we have no control) like biting our nails, or losing our tempers, not to speak of the smoking habit, or coffee drinking habit. The

NLP way of dealing with such a situation is as follows. First identify the habit you want to change. Second, identify what you actually see, internally, just before you get into the behaviour you dislike. It would be better to engage in that behaviour and, as you do it, generate an associated picture of it. Since the picture is associated the feeling of unpleasantness or dislike will also occur. Third, create a dissociated picture of the outcome you seek. Fourth, switch these two pictures in this way: Start by seeing the first associated picture, big and bright. Then insert a small dark dissociated picture of the outcome you desire in the lower right corner. Next interchange the two pictures in an instant, so that the small dark picture will grow big and bright and will cover the first picture, which should dim and shrink into nothingness. Then blank out the screen and open your eyes.

Repeat the switching procedure five times making sure that you blank out the screen each time you complete it. Lastly, try again to generate the first picture. If your procedure has been effective you will find this task difficult. The picture will tend to vanish and be replaced by the second picture.

Although this by no means exhausts the repertoire of what NLP is capable of achieving, if you have an adventurous introspective spirit and patience to try out its techniques, you will go far. Here is the outline of a new behaviour generator you can use: 1) Select a situation in which the new behaviour is desired, say, a meeting where you wish to speak eloquently; 2) Pick a model who excels in this behaviour; 3) Watch and listen, in your own mind, to the model behaving in the situation; 4) Substitute your image and voice for the model's; 5) Step into the movie, to make it an associated experience and experience the body feeling; 6) Future pace, that is, give yourself a cue, something like bringing three of your fingers together, to trigger the new behaviour. Practise it often enough and eventually you should become as good as your model.

Just in case you can't think of a model to emulate, nor of

any limiting belief you wish to change, here is a daily meditation you can use to achieve your full potential. Keep aside 15 to 20 minutes after you go to bed every night before you actually sleep. Lie down on your back. Relax all your muscles and take three deep breaths. Then state to yourself: "My subconscious will do whatever is necessary to make me behave as farsightedly, gracefully, assertively and creatively as I am capable of in every activity of my life." Then count backwards from 300 to 1. Most people fall asleep long before they reach 1. If you do so, too, fine. If you lose count somewhere along the way but don't fall asleep begin again wherever you think you may have lost count. If you reach 1 before you fall asleep, repeat the statement you began with and then you are free to sleep. Bandler assures you that your behaviour will evolve to greater maturity and effectiveness, if you repeat the formula nightly.

Most of the above exercises are conditioning exercises. NLP can also be used for deconditioning. In an article titled 'Beyond Self,' NLP practitioner Richard Bolstad models Krishnamurti's insight with the help of well - established NLP approaches. Below is a summary printed here by permission of the author.

In modelling the teachings Krishnamurti, Richard Bolstad came upon a clear exposition of how, in NLP terms, the illusion of self is maintained, and consequently how it comes to an end. For NLP practitioners Krishnamurti's work provides a series of recognisable NLP processes for unveiling the secret all humanity has been seeking. Bolstad introduces four central "experiments" to use Krishnamurti's term; four processes which lead immediately to the experience of that which is beyond self.

A New Definition of the Self

The "Self" is a nominalisation of a process which we could call "owning" or "appropriating" or "identifying", according to Bolstad: Information flows into our neurology via the five senses from outside, from other areas in the neurology, and also as part of the various non-sensory connections between all aspects of life. There is a very simple mechanism by which, from moment to moment, our thinking then divides this information into two sets. I see the door and I think "not-me". I see my hand and I think "me" (I "appropriate" the hand to myself, or "own" it; I "identify" with it). Or, internally I see the craving for chocolate and I think "not-me". I see the ability to read this article and understand it and I think "me" (again, I appropriate or own it; I identify with it). Actually, all these pieces of information are in one mind! The notion of self and non-self is an arbitrary division; a metaprogramme or internal sort similar to matching or mismatching. This division may be useful metaphorically, but it is a division which has "taken over" and now thinks it runs the neurology.

Like any metaprogramme or internal sort, the owning of experiences as "me" and the disowning of experiences as "not me" occurs largely unconsciously, but is continuously active. The whole notion of strategies as used in NLP depends on appropriating or owning one sensory experience after another in a sequence. A vast array of sensory experiences is available at every moment, and the metaprogramme of owning selects out one section at a time as "mine". It seems, for example, as if "I" am first holding a book, and then "I" am looking at the words, and then "I" am saying the words to myself, and then "I" am making pictures of the meaning. Actually, all of the senses are functioning all of the time, but conscious attention is shifting from one sense to another as the sense of "I" appropriates or identifies with each sense in turn.

Attention is not Concentration

Krishnamurti explains "When thought identifies itself with sensation, then it becomes the 'me'.... To observe with all your senses — in that there is no identification. The question is, can you look with all your senses awakened?.... When there is movement of thought, then it is one particular sense operating. Can I find out if there is a totally different dimension? A state where consciousness as we know it ceases.... This is only possible when the sensory as identification with thought is understood. Then the senses do not produce the psychological structure, as the 'me'"

So Krishnamurti says, according to Bolstad, simply being aware of all of the senses at once puts an end to the process of owning/identifying. Here is the answer to a double bind which many students of "meditation" have been caught in. Students of meditation have often assumed that the ending of thought (particularly of Auditory digital representations) is the prerequisite for experiencing a state beyond sorrow.

One solution to the difficulty of ending thought has been to take the attention which has been wandering down various paths, and hold it in one sensory system (in Zen this is done by concentrating on the breath, for example). Krishnamurti argues that this leads to concentration, but not to awareness. It focuses the sense of self, but does not end it. Put in NLP terms, it may give your self a better strategy, but it does take you beyond strategies. Krishnamurti says "I am interested in so-called meditation but my thoughts are distracted, so I fix my mind on a picture, an image, or an idea and exclude all other thoughts.... A business man making money is very concentrated — he may even be ruthless, putting aside every other feeling and concentrating completely on what he wants. A man who is interested in anything is naturally, spontaneously concentrated. Such concentration is not meditation, it is merely exclusion.... A man who is fully aware is meditating.... Then you can follow, without condemnation or justification [owning or disowning], every movement of thought and feeling; by following every thought and every feeling as it arises you bring about tranquillity which is not compelled, not regimented, but which is the outcome of having no problem, no contradiction. It is like the pool that becomes peaceful, quiet, any evening when there is no wind; when the mind is still, then that which is immeasurable comes into being."

In terms of the sensory systems, as described in NLP, meditation simply means the simultaneous awakening of all the senses. "If you are so attending, all your senses are completely awake. It is not one sense attending, but the totality of all the senses. Otherwise you cannot attend. Complete sensory activity is a state of attention. Partial sensory activity leads to concentration....Can one see completely with all the senses? See not with the eyes alone, but with the ears; to listen, to taste to touch?.... Watch yourself one day. Look at the sunlight and see whether you can see with all your senses, completely awake and completely free. Which leads to an interesting fact. Where there is disharmony, there is the self. Attention is complete harmony. There must be a great volume of energy gathered through harmony. It is like the river Ganga. Attention is a movement to eternity."

Exercise One: Differentiating the Senses

In order to awaken the senses, Krishnamurti points out, I must first be able to differentiate which sensory modality is active. It has been known for some time that when a person trained in music listens to an orchestra, a different area of their brain is activated than when a person with no training listens (the expert is identifying the musical instruments used and the structure of the music etc. often using visual construct instead of auditory). When a person listens to a language they know, a different area of the brain is used than when they listen to one they don't (auditory digital versus auditory). Krishnamurti says "Can you see a tree without the operation of thought, without the image of the tree? — the image being the thought that says: that is an oak. In observing a tree what takes place? There is the space between the observer and the tree, there is distance; then there is the botanical knowledge [Auditory digital], the like or dislike of that tree [Kinesthetic]. I have an image of a tree [visual construct] and that image looks at the tree.... Is there an observation without the interference of thought?

—that means without the interference of any image. You can find this out; it's not a question of just accepting or believing. You can look at your wife or your husband, the tree, the cloud, or the person sitting next to you, without any image."

For this first exercise, then, just be aware of some specific thing (a tree, for example) and find out which senses are activated. Listen to hear if you name the tree, and then stop naming it, and look at it and listen to it without knowing intellectually what it is, and without comparing it to other images internally.

Exercise Two: Awakening the Senses

This is very simple to experience. Take a moment now to actually see the book in front of you. Don't name it as "book" or you'll end up staying in Auditory Digital and talking to yourself about attention (ie keep the senses clearly differentiated). Instead, just see the shape of the book. Expand your vision out, so that while seeing these words you are also seeing all else in your visual field. Now hear the sounds around you as you read; even the sounds of your own body, as you see all that you can see. Now add the tastes in your mouth, and the smells in your nose, and the feelings of your body, both inside and on the skin. Continue seeing, hearing, smelling, tasting, feeling. Allow all the senses to be awake at one time.

Shortly, you may have found that your attention became concentration again, as you, for example, thought about what you were doing. As soon as you notice that, attention is there again, so allow all the senses to reawaken. There is no need to attempt to keep attention "constant". In fact, attempting to keep attention constant, like attempting to do anything else, is identifying or owning (ie losing attention). It is the activity of the self. Each time, as your senses awaken, the illusion of the self disappears. As this is not a form of concentration, it need not be done in a certain posture. This exercise can be done throughout daily life, and returned to whenever one notices its absence. Krishnamurti urges not to treat it as a task. He also says "You cannot watch from morning till night. You cannot be vigilant, never blinking for the whole day. So play with it. Play with it lightly."

Dealing With Unpleasant States

One of the first challenges that people may come across when using the process of Awakening the Senses is that of unpleasant states. The temptation is to shift the attention away from these and thus begin the whole process of "disowning" or excluding them, ie of the self. Krishnamurti had an interesting model of how people maintain negative internal states. He held that painful states persist because the person has built a neurological barrier around the states, preventing them from "flowering" in a natural way, and dying like any flower, so that the next state emerges. The self actually causes suffering! Rather than try to solve the immediate problem a person raised with him, Krishnamurti would invite them to deal with this underlying dynamic. For example, questioned about how a teacher could deal with frustration in a student, he replied "How do you question so that frustration unfolds, so that frustration flowers? It is only when thought flowers that it can naturally die. Like the flower in a garden, thought must blossom, it must come to fruition and then it dies."

His own student, Pupul Jayakar, describes Krishnamurti's technique for this. It is reminiscent of several NLP patterns. In the following quote, note that Jayakar uses the word 'thought' where NLP would use 'State': "He would lead you from thought to thought, till there was an ending of thought. He would do this, for example, with the thought of greed. He would do this with a rising of fear. He would keep on saying, 'And then what arises? And then what arises?' so that you started observing, 'what is', as it arose. You also observed, 'what should be' as it arose in thought. So that one was awake in that instant of 'what is'."

Krishnamurti explains "To say that jealousy is the cause of

attachment is mere verbalisation. But, in actually allowing jealousy to flower, the fact that you are attached to something becomes a fact, an emotional fact, not an intellectual verbal idea. And so each flowering reveals what you have not been able to discover; and as each fact unveils itself, it flowers and you deal with it. You let the fact flower and it opens other doors, till there is no flowering at all of any kind and, therefore, no cause or motive of any kind."

Exercise Three: Ascending States

Identify a significant emotional state which you may have resisted and prevented from flowering and ending. Be aware of that state, and check, as you're aware of that, that you allow it to flower, as if you were watching a flower rise up and die down again. Now ask yourself, "What arises from underneath that?" Be aware of that next state as it too flowers and dies down, and check again, what arises. Continue until you have run through to a state where there is no new distress which arises; until there is the pure ground of awareness again. At this point, people tend to report an extraordinary feeling of joy, of love, of oneness with whatever is.

The Deeper Layers of Mind

A second challenge which may arise as a person continues to experiment with awakening the senses is that the self may learn how to go "underground", and attention turn back into undifferentiated Auditory digital introspection. In a discussion with world respected physicist Dr. David Bohm, Krishnamurti discusses this issue.

Bohm : That is always the trouble. Everybody gets into this trouble: that he seems to be looking at everything, at his problems, saying, "Those are my problems, I am looking." But that looking is only thinking, but it is confused with looking ... that means the operation of thought is unconscious for the most part and therefore one doesn't know it is going on. We may say consciously we have realised that all this has to be changed, it has to be different.

Krishnamurti : But it is still going on unconsciously. So can you talk to my unconscious, knowing my conscious brain is going to resist you? Because you are telling me something which is revolutionary, you are telling me something which shatters my whole house which I have built so careful, and I won't listen to you - you follow? In my instinctive reactions I push you away. So you realise that and say, "Look, all right, old friend, just don't bother to listen to me. I am going to talk to your unconscious. I am going to talk to your unconscious and make that unconscious see ... . That changes me, not all this verbalisation ...

Bohm : to reach the unconscious you have to have an action which doesn't directly appeal to the conscious.

Krishnamurti : Yes. That is affection, that is love. When you talk to my waking consciousness, it is hard, clever, subtle, brittle. And you penetrate that, penetrate it with your look, with your affection, with all the feeling you have. That operates. Not anything else."

And again "What is needed is a radical change in the unconscious. Any conscious action of the will cannot touch the unconscious. As the conscious will cannot touch the unconscious pursuits, wants, urges, the conscious mind must subside, be still, and not try to force the unconscious, according to any particular pattern of action. The unconscious has its own pattern of action, its own frame within which it functions. This frame cannot be broken by any outward action, and will is an outward act. If this is really seen and understood, the outward mind is still; and because there is no resistance set up by will, one will find that the so - called unconscious begins to free itself from its own limitations. Then only is there a radical transformation in the total being of man."

This is a principle well understood in NLP. If the self operates both consciously and "unconsciously" then to end the process of the self requires an action at the unconscious level. Krishnamurti calls this deeper action love. Love comes upon one when one suddenly discovers the beauty of a sunset, or a symphony, or a gentle touch. "There is beauty only when your heart and mind know what love is. Without love and that sense of beauty there is no virtue, and you know very well that, do what you will, improve society, feed the poor, you will only be creating more mischief, for without Love there is only ugliness and poverty in your own heart and mind. But when there is love, and beauty, whatever you do is right, whatever you do is in order. If you know how to love, then you can do what you like because it will solve all other problems. So we reach the point: can the mind come upon love without discipline, without thought, without enforcement, without any book, any teacher or leader — come upon it as one comes upon a lovely sunset? ... But you don't know how to come to this extraordinary fount — so what do you do? If you don't know what to do, you do nothing, don't you? Absolutely nothing. Then inwardly you are completely silent. Do you understand what that means? It means that you are not seeking, not wanting, not pursuing; there is no centre at all. Then there is love."

Exercise Four: Unconscious Transformation

The teachings of people such as Krishnamurti are designed to awaken this unconscious movement. That process has already begun, because as Krishnamurti points out, the first step is the last. There is no path to enlightenment. There is only a single act: to wake up! As you read these words, the act has already taken place. It may not yet be continuous, but then nothing is continuous. There is only this moment, and in this moment you can see, hear, feel, smell, and taste the life that is. That is all.

Love, as Krishnamurti says, may be the answer to all our problems. But to find it, the "me" that wants to find it must be still. Pupul Jayakar asked Krishnamurti what the essence of his teachings was. He said "Where you are, the other is not!" And yet that other is the source of all that has been beautiful in your life, of all happiness, of all meaning. It is for the other that we live. The metaprogram of the self is constantly seeking continuity, through "owning" both experiences and things. And through this owning, one hopes to possess joy, love, beauty and truth.

In an article 'The Unanswerable Question,' NLP practitioners, Dr. Richard Bolstad and Margot Hamblett analyse a basic insight from Krishnamurti. Below is a summary printed by permission of Dr. Bolstad.

Spiritual teachers throughout history have guided their students from their initial, external, answerable questions, to the one place where true answers abide. In this article the authors model the work of teachers from the Hindu and Buddhist traditions, and of twentieth century teacher Jiddu Krishnamurti. This article is about finding that place where you ask an unanswerable question. As NLP continues to demonstrate, attaining such states is not a mystic privilege of the few. It is freely available to us all.

Finding the Right Question

Asking the unanswerable question is a very factual and practical process. Oscar Wilde pointed out that, in ordinary speech, "a practical scheme is one already in existence or which could be carried out under the existing conditions" He adds that if we want to change the existing conditions, such schemes are foolish in the extreme. And yet, being trapped by the familiar, our questions have usually tended to be limited too. A questioner once asked Jiddu Krishnamurti "Can you ever empty this storehouse of impressions which you have had?" Here is his reply:

Krishnamurti: You've put a wrong question. It is a wrong question because you say 'Can you ever.' Who is the 'you' and what do you mean by 'ever'? Which means.... Is it possible? Sirs, look, we never put the impossible question — we are always putting the question of what is possible. If you put an impossible question, your mind then has to find the answer in terms of the impossible — not of what is possible. All the great scientific discoveries are based on this, the impossible. It was impossible to go to the moon. But if you say, 'It is possible' then you drop it. Because it was impossible, three hundred thousand people co-operated and worked at it, night and day — they put their mind to it and went to the moon. But we never put the impossible question! The impossible question is this: can the mind empty itself of the known? — itself, not you empty the mind. That is an impossible question. If you put it with tremendous earnestness, with seriousness, with passion, you'll find out. But if you say, 'Oh, it is possible', then you are stuck...

Who is The "You" That Wants to Change?

Krishnamurti's common response when someone asked him how to change something was to ask them "Who is the you who wants to change?" For example, when someone asks him about death, he says "If you do not understand what you are actually, not descriptively, then death becomes a dreadful thing. If we are to go into the question of death, we must understand what you are: a name, a form, man or woman, with certain qualities, certain tendencies, idiosyncracies, desire, pain, anxiety, uncertainty, confusion. Out of this confusion, you invent something permanent — the Absolute, the Brahman or God. But what you actually are, is the movement of thought. That thought may invent the idea that you have got the spark of divinity in you, but it is still the movement of thought. So what are you apart from your physical reactions, differently educated, rich and poor? Actually, when you look at yourself, what are you? Aren't you all this? If there is something permanent in you, then why seek permanence in something else? Do you understand my question? As we said, begin with uncertainty, begin with not-knowing. This is what you are."

In the previous passage 'Beyond Self' the nature of the "Self" was discussed. From an NLP perspective, as pointed out there, the self is a nominalisation of the process of "owning" experiences; it is a style of thinking rather than a "thing". It was noted that spiritual teachers have again and again identified this "owning" process as the source of suffering. Krishnamurti points out that from childhood we build up an image (NLP would say an internal representation) of our "self" and it is this image which is hurt when we feel hurt. "If one has an image about oneself and another comes along and says: don't be an idiot, one gets hurt. The image which has been built about oneself as not being an idiot is "me" and that gets hurt.... When there is total attention to the statement that one is an idiot it has totally lost all significance. Because when there is attention there is not a centre which is reacting."

Like Krishnamurti, other teachers have recommended the seeker enquire first and last into who they are. The great twentieth century Hindu teacher Ramana Maharshi also focused his entire method on this one question "Who am I?" He says "In this method, the final question is the only one and is raised from the very beginning.... Since every other thought can occur only after the rise of the "I"-thoughts, and since the mind is nothing but a bundle of thoughts, it is only through the enquiry "Who am I?" that the mind subsides. Moreover, the integral "I" thought implicit in such enquiry, having destroyed all other thoughts, itself finally gets destroyed or consumed, just as a stick used for stirring the burning funeral pyre gets consumed."

What Next?

Krishnamurti describes the way that asking the unanswerable question actively alters the person's experience as they ask it. He says "Actually, what are you? Have you ever asked it, and have you found an answer? Is there an answer? If there is an answer, it is not in terms of what you already know. But what you know is the past, and the past is time; and the time is not 'you'. The 'you' is changing.... When I put that question to find out what I am, that 'what I am' is always in the past. The 'me' is always the past. I can only put the question and enquire into something static. And through the thing that is dead, that is static, the past, I have to find out what I am; and so fear never goes away. But fear goes away the moment I put that question and watch myself all the time, not direct my attention to the past but actually to what is taking place, which is 'the me' that is alive."

As you'll find out in following the Unanswerable Question process below, this simple question leads to a profound experience, once attention shifts from an "image" of the self remembered from the past, to a search for the self in the present "now". At first, one discovers that the internal representations of "self" that one has are only representations. In fact, there can be no answer, if one asks the question in the present moment. At the moment this is understood, no representation arises in response to the question at all. There is total blankness, total silence, total stillness. No struggle was needed to reach this moment. Maharshi explains "Instead of setting about saying there is a mind and I want to kill it, you begin to seek its source, and then you find it does not exist at all." In that state, extraordinary change occurs. This is not a state of despair, of "giving up", all of which would imply the response of the same mechanism which has been collecting. It is a state of complete stillness.

At this stage, an observer may wonder what the person is supposed to "do" next to reach these "extraordinary experiences". But as Maharshi cautions about the ending of the self, "All that you need do is to find out its origin and stay there. Your effort can extend only so far. Then the beyond will take care of itself. You are helpless there. No effort can reach it." Explaining why the "self" cannot think up some smart plan to solve things and find this "other" experience, Krishnamurti says simply "Where you are, the other is not!"

Unanswerable Questions Break free From Set "Attractors"

The most amusing thing about our normal "answerable" questions is that we so easily think they are evidence of our "freedom of thought". Krishnamurti contrasts the state of "choice" and the state of freedom. A person who is choosing is choosing between two things which they already know about, which they already have internal representations of. Freedom, on the other hand, occurs when something totally new occurs, something that is not within the field that the person operated in before. When a lion is kept in a cage, it paces back and forth from one end of the cage to the other. After a few years, the cage can be removed, and for some time the lion will still pace back and forth in its prescribed area. It has no doubt become very proud of its ability to choose which place it wants to be in. If you tried to reason with it, you might say "Don't choose between here and there! That's not freedom. You could be anywhere, but you limit yourself to such a small range. This "choice" is irrelevant. Simply move where you will." The lion would quite likely become very suspicious at such attempts to take away its "freedom of choice".

Putting aside his unfortunate use of male language, the point can be seen very clearly in this following passage from Krishnamurti: "We are talking about the radical change of human behaviour so that man is not self-centred as he is, which is causing such great destruction in the world. If one is aware, then we can begin to ask whether that conditioning can be totally changed so that man is completely free. Now, he thinks he is free to do what he likes. Each individual thinks he can do what he likes, all over the world, and his freedom is based on choice because he can choose where to live, what kind of work he can do, choose between this idea and that idea, this ideal or that ideal, change from one god to another god, from one guru to another, from one philosopher to another. This capacity to choose brings in the concept of freedom, but in the totalitarian state there is no freedom; you can't do what you want to do. It is totally controlled. Choice is not freedom. Choice is merely moving in the same field from one corner to another. Is this clear? Our brain being limited, we are asking, is it possible for the brain to free itself so that there is no fear? Then there is right relationship with all the neighbours in the world."

In the new science of non-linear systems (Chaos theory), choice would be described as the result of an "attractor". Chaos theory points out that most natural systems are exceedingly complex, and cannot be explained or even measured in any detail. But they none - the - less have certain basic predictabilities about them. For example, all snowflakes are different, but all of them have a "six-sided-ness". Six-sided-ness is an attractor for snowflakes. The shapes vary, but they never vary beyond the basic attractor. However, in certain extreme circumstances, a snowflake slips out of this attractor. It then becomes a raindrop, following a totally different set of rules. To take another example of an attractor, every oak tree is unique, but if you learn what the attractor is like (the "essence" or genetic mark of an oak tree) you can recognise that they are all oaks. Another example is that, in terms of the earth's climate, there are two known attractors. One is what we have now; a balance that supports life, even when we pour greenhouse gasses into the atmosphere for a century. Though the weather varies unpredictably from year to year, it none-the-less stays within certain limits. The other known possible attractor for the Earth's system would be where the seas freeze, and the land is covered in ice. That too would be a stable attractor. Scientists do not know why the current climatic attractor is holding out; the other state, called the White Earth Equilibrium, is mathematically just as likely.

Spiritual teachers have sought to bring their students to a change which is so fundamental that it breaks out of the attractor of the self. Answerable questions cannot do that. They ask only within the presupposed limits of selfhood. When the questioner above asked Krishnamurti "Can 'I' ever empty this storehouse of impressions?" he asked a question which presupposed the continued existence of the self. In fact, the more the questioner tried to empty the storehouse, the more the storehouse (through its agent; his own "self") would remain full. The more "he" acts, the more life stays the same. Krishnamurti recommended he ask first "Who is the 'I' that wants this emptied?", and then "Can this storehouse of impressions empty itself?". These, as he notes, are questions which the "self" cannot answer. That is why they are worth asking. When the questioner is still, then the other comes into being.

What is Change?

From the perspective of that stillness, that silence which comes when the unanswerable question is finally heard, our old problems seem rather insignificant. They look like an illusory cage that we once paced around in. Once you understand this, you will want to return to that silent place more frequently to experience that freedom. This practice is known in the East as meditation. This is simply another way to describe the same place which we reach by the Ascending States process.

Of course, there are still many things which "you" may wonder. You may ask, "Do I have the right to guide someone else through this?" Krishnamurti's answer is simple. "Please listen; do not agree, but listen to find out. We have to be both the teacher and the disciple. The meaning of that word 'disciple' is he who learns. Also we must be the teacher. The very act of learning gives us the responsibility to teach."

And you may ask "What is the other? What will be here when 'I' am not?". Here is Krishnamurti's response. "Only when you totally deny the known — what you know, your experiences, your knowledge (not the technological knowledge but the knowledge of your ambitions, your experiences, your family) — when you deny the known completely, when you wipe it away, when you die to all that, you will see that there is an extraordinary emptiness, an extraordinary space in the mind. And it is only that space that knows what it is to love. And it is only in that space there is creation- not the creation of children or putting a painting on the canvas, but that creation which is the total energy, the unknowable. But to come to that, you must die to everything you have known. And in that dying there is great beauty, there is inexhaustible life-energy."

And with this love, with this vast energy and creativity, we turn to look once more at the things in our life that were once "problems" for which we sought solutions. And find that these "problems" are no more. "If you seek, then the search becomes a problem.... If you are alive, really alive every minute, then it does not become a problem; but there is a constant regard, a constant look, which is the response, not of memory but of something much more, much wider, deeper."

The Unanswerable Question: An Example

Modelled as an NLP process, then, the Unanswerable Question solves problems not simply by altering our perception of the problem, but by removing our "self" from the perceptual process. A script for the process follows. Here is an example of its use, with George, who sought help because of longstanding conflict with one of his children.

Richard : So George, think of yourself in that situation you want to change. What feelings do you have there?

George : I feel tense and worried when I'm with him. Kind of guilty and even confused. I can't work out what to do.

Richard : Now, you say you want to change that situation. Who is the you that wants to change that?

George : What do you mean? It's just me.

Richard : How do you see, hear or feel that "just you" you say you are there?

George : I see me tense and frowning like I do in when I'm with him.

Richard : As you think of that you, tense and frowning like you do when you're with him, who are you that is aware of that thought now?

George : Well, I'm sort of an observer; I'm a kind of compassionate observer.

Richard : How do you see, hear or feel that kind of compassionate observer you say you are there.

George : I see me smiling gently.

Richard : As you think of that you smiling gently in that way now, who are you, that's aware of that thought.

George : A stillness.

Richard : How do you see, hear or feel that stillness?

George : Space, like outer space, very still.

Richard : As you think of that outer space very still in that way now, who are you, that is aware of that thought?

George : Life. Everything.

Richard : How do you see hear or feel that life, that everything?

George : The universe, the stars.

Richard : As you think of that universe, the stars in that way now, who are you, that is aware of that thought?

George : Shrugs and smiles.

Richard : And just be aware as that question becomes unanswerable. Having found this state, just be aware; listening, seeing, feeling, tasting, smelling, with all the senses awake. [George nods] Staying in this state, be aware of the universe, the stars. Is it there? [nod] How does this original state change the universe, the stars?

George : It seems even vaster.

Richard : Staying in this state, be aware of that outer space very still. Is it there? [nod] How does this state change that outer space, very still?

George : It's just more so.

Richard : Staying in this state, be aware of that you smiling gently. Is it there?

George : I don't think so.

Richard : So, staying in this state, be aware of that you tense and frowning. Is it there?

George : It's gone.

Richard : So how does being in this state change the process occurring in the situation which that first "you" wanted to change?

George : Well it feels like I have access to everything. I am everything.

Richard : And how does it change the way you feel there?

George : I feel immense calmness and love.

The Effects of the Process, in NLP Terms

The authors have used this process with quite a large number of people, and most describe it as a dramatic experience. Some people say that when the question becomes unanswerable, they feel as if something exploded in their mind, or that they know what the Japanese meant by saying this process causes Satori (sudden enlightenment). The state that the person enters is quite variable, because the technique is not specifically designed to create a state change per se. It is designed to create a radical shift in perceptual position. Some people describe the state they then enter as calm and detached. Some describe it as euphoric and blissful. These are "individual" responses to the central perceptual shift. So far everyone who gets this perceptual shift has then reported that their "problem" was solved. Most find themselves unable to access their previous problem state at all.

The authors have found it useful to explain to the person that the question will, at some point, become unanswerable. This gives less surprise to that moment, but the shift is the same. Without explanation, some people become a little unnerved at the point where they discover that there is no "them" observing.

Anyone can ask the unanswerable question. To others, your question may seem simple. But an innocent tubmaker or a devout monk are both only a fraction of a centimetre away from their original state. Who is to say which conversation is more noble. That which is beyond all self, that which holds the universe in the palm of its hand, waits for you now, at this moment. You have only to ask, and it is there. And where it is, you are not....

But who are you?

Spiritual Intelligence

Through a perceptual process which he variously terms 'sensing', 'observing', 'watching' and 'choiceless awareness' Krishnamurti shows how you can access what he calls 'creative intelligence'. This intelligence is deeper than and different from rational intelligence which is usually measured through IQ tests. Fr. Paul Edwards, therapist and counsellor, terms this deeper intelligence 'spiritual intelligence'. He analyses it in his book the spiritual intelligence handbook.

Spiritual intelligence for Fr. Edwards is like the intelligence of a genius. " A genius is born not made. It does not matter how much or how little they know, they are always geniuses. Their genius can never be taken away from them. Like genius, spiritual intelligence is a way of perceiving. We are all born with it, live with it, and use it. It can never be taken from us. Yet many have not named it and do not have a conscious choice when they use it."

Spiritual intelligence, Fr. Edwards asserts is a scientific fact. " It is true that when you are feeling secure, at peace, loved and are happy, you will see, hear and act differently than when you are feeling insecure, unhappy and unloved. We all have an inner peace which we can access by using our conscious spiritual perception. This is not something you tell others about. You must show them how to do it."

The key is that you cannot access the inner peace through rational, judgemental and analytical thinking. You have to change to see the unseen by using your conscious sensing, discerning awareness of spiritual perception the challenge is to get the people out of the rational way of thinking into the way of spiritual perception before trying to enter the inner peace.

"The missing link for me was to start by actually experiencing the presence of anything," Edwards discloses. "You can close your eyes and feel each other by sensing their presence. You don't really have to close your eyes but you must change from your rational/analytical faculty to your conscious spiritual faculty. And closing your eyes seems to help."

In order to feel the presence of anything by sensing start with something familiar, he advises. From there it doesn't take but a moment to sense the presence of the inner peace.

Psychology of Mind

Similar to Fr. Edwards approach is the approach based on a set of principles known as the Psychology of Mind which was initially inspired by a man called Syd Banks and was formulated into a psychology by Dr. Roger Mills and Dr. George Pransky, author of *The Renaissance of Psychology*. This principles are best explained in the bestselling book, *Slowing Down to the Speed of Life:How to Create a More Peaceful Simpler Life from the Inside Out* by Richard Carlson and Joseph Bailey. They write:

Thought is the power that creates human experience – the ultimate force that creates, shapes, and transforms our lives. We create our experience of life through our thinking we can't have an experience without thought... What we think becomes our emotions, perceptions, sensations, decisions, behavior... These thoughts, and so many others have the capacity to rob our mental health in any given moment. And because we believe that these outside circumstances create our feelings, most of us try to restore our mental health from the outside by altering those circumstances — taking a tranquilizer to relax, throwing a temper tantrum, buying another time saving device or quitting our job. If we believe that our feelings are determined by outside forces, it follows that we will seek something equally external in response. As we gain an understanding of our psychological experience however, we can recognise that the actual *source* of our experience is always our thinking. Thus we can begin to restore the power in our life...

Although thought creates all experience, thought may proceed in two very different ways and modes. When you know what mode of thinking you are in, you are in a position to leave in a healthy psychological functioning.

The first mode, *the processing mode* resembles the way a computer processes information... We will refer to it by the terms processing mode, process thing, analytical thinking and computer thinking. The processing mode of thought performs the following functions: 1) stores information (memory); 2) it analysis this data (sorts it, compares it to existing information and organises it into beliefs , concepts and ideas.); 3) it plans our lives (creates a simulation of the future based on past memories and our imagination; 4) it computes and calculates existing data in our memory in order to organise our lives and respond to situations; 5) it remembers information that we have previously learnt.

This analytical mode of thinking is essential to living our lives effectively. It allow us to learn everything from language to mathematics. With its help we can operate a computer drive a car, ... remember our name... and we can do a million other tasks that once learnt are easily repeated.

The down side of this mode of thinking is that we don't know all the variables, we continue to churn inside; we obsess about and rethink problems without result—a draining, frustrating and stressful process...

The other way of thinking we have available to us operates

like a river It is always flowing bringing us new infromation and thoughts in the moment — some from memory, some from the creative source. We call this mode of thinking the free flowing mode... When we are in flow thinking, we experience thought as effortless. Or thinking is in the moment, responsive to whatever is happening or needed at the time... When we are in the flow, thoughts seem to come to us out of the blue. Thinking takes no effort. In fact, effort will block our flow thinking and place us right back in the processing mode. Most people love it when they are in the free flowing mode, but few know how to gain access to it dependably.

You will notice that these two modes of thinking function in discreet ways you are either in one or the other... there is nothing in between. In the processing mode it feels as if you are thinking, since processing takes concentration and effort... By clearing your mind, your automatically go into the free flowing mode, where your thought flow from one to the next without effort in an intelligent though diffused manner.

Another way to put this is to say that if you are actively thinking you are in the processing mode. If you are passively thinking you are in the free flowing mode. When you are in the flow it feels as if you are not thinking at all. The thinking seems to happen through you. Free-flowing mode thinking moves naturally constantly bringing you fresh harmonious thoughts. When you are in the processing mode, however, the thinking is originating from memory.

So how do you access these two modes? We are most familiar with the processing/analytical mode only because it is the mode of thinking that we have been thought to value the most. Whenever we actually feel that we are thinking, we are in the processing mode. It can feel effortful, as if we are bearing down on a subject. It can feel stressful if we misuse it or stay in that mode too long...

To access the free-flowing mode we must go of our analytical thinking. We clear the mind. Clearing the mind is much like letting the silt settle in water. You do nothing and the silt automatically settles. Anything you do to try to settle the silt actually keeps it stirred up. Another way of thinking about it is to take a problem and put it on the back burner; that is, don't actively think about it, but choose to momentarily forget it so that flow thinking can go to work on it while you clean your house or putter in the garden or answer phone calls. To gain access to original thought you must first know that it exists and you must value the power of it. Second, we must have faith that if we do clear the mind this mode will automatically start feeding us a flow of thoughts — which it will. It may give us answers we were not expecting but they will be far superior to and wiser than thoughts we have already gone over in the mind. As we said earlier flow thinking is better for finding an unknown solution process thinking can gain access only to memory data. By letting go of the analytical, trying-to-figure-it–out mode, we create a vacuum that the free-flowing mode can fill.

Not knowing, that is, being willing to admit that we don't know, is one of the keys that opens the door to creative intelligence. It takes humility to open that door. Our ego does not like not knowing and would prefer to go over and over what we already think and believe rather than trust in a subtle, unknown process like creative intelligence. But opening ourselves to the unknown is a peaceful productive alternative to our business-as-usual processing mode where we pretend (or hope) that we know what is going on. By clearing the mind and admitting to ourselves that we don't know, we receive answers that are often brilliant, unexpected, and just right for the situation.

Unconditional Bliss

In his book *Unconditional Bliss: Finding Happiness in the Face of Hardship, (New Age Books)* Howard Raphael Cushnir unveils another perceptual process that mirrors Krishnamurti's and may be helpful for those having difficulty in accessing his insights. It is a simple two-step process called Living the

Questions. Cushnir writes that when we face anything unwanted or unpleasant we feel a contraction or constriction in our body. On the other hand when we are contented and blissful we feel a bodily expansion. To turn the contraction into expansion we have to ask the two questions Cushnir talks about:

1) What is happening right now?
2) Can I be with it?

You ask the question 'what is happening right now?' and await a reply from within. The answer will come in some form of explanation. Then you ask the second question 'Can I be with it?', that is, can I fully accept this explanation and live with its facts. You will probably get another reply implying either resistance to the acceptance of the situation or its unconditional acceptance. In case of the former, that is, if you are resisting within yourself the cause of the contraction, try to distance yourself from that resistance and watch it, recognizing it is there. Then again put yourself that question 'What is happening right now?' The answer now could be different from the earlier answer to the same question, in which case the answer to the second question 'Can I be with it?' could be yes. In which case the contraction in your body would have given way to its expansion and you would be feeling blissful.

It is easier to analyse the situation with a concrete example. For example I am feeling constricted and ask my self the question 'What is happening right now?'

I reply : I am stuck in traffic. I am late for a meeting. I am pounding the horn. I am shouting. I hate this.

I ask the question 'Can I be with it?'

My reply : No. My cell phone is dead so I can't call. I'll lose the account. I'll lose my job.

Again I ask : 'What is happening right now?'

Reply : 'I am flooded with anxiety. Fear. Frustration. Why did this have to happen? Why today? I woke up feeling so great.(The feeling of contraction is becoming more pronounced.)

I again ask : 'Can I be with it?'

I reply : No! I've got to get there! May be I should try a short cut or park and catch a bus or just run.(I am becoming aware of my resistance to accepting what is happening.)

I ask again 'What is happening right now?'

Reply : I've done it again. Left the house too late. Sabotaged myself like Dad always did. (I am analysing the situation.)

So again I ask the same question:What is happening right now?

Reply : I am making a mountain out of a mole hill. Getting all worked up about something I can't change. (I am judging. Trying to figure out what is wrong.)

I again ask the question: 'What is happening right now?'

Reply : You know what... I hate feeling so awful. So out of control. But may be if I give in for a few minutes I can get rid of it. (I am bargaining, trying to make it go away.)

I again ask the question: 'What is happening right now?'

Reply : My heart is pounding and my mind is racing. I am sweating. My knuckles are white of the wheel.

Now I ask: 'Can I be with it?'

Reply : You mean, just feel all this? Stop trying to push it away or think my way out of it. I guess so. I mean I'll try. (This is the beginning of acceptance.)

Again I ask: What is happening right now?

Reply : Wow! It's totally raging through me. Like a fire. I feel panic and frustration everywhere. Overwhelming me.

Again I ask the question: Can I be with it?

Reply : I don't know. It's so strong. But ... wait. It is starting to subside a little. Hey, I think it is passing. I mean, I am still a little anxious... But I am also relaxing. (I am feeling a release).

Again the question: What is happening right now?

Reply : I am stuck in traffic. Plain and simple. I guess I can be with it. And bliss? Who knows. But there is something liberating about staying so open. (I feel the blissful expansion.)

There is a possible alternative to asking these two questions when you feel constricted. It is just telling yourself I shall not try to understand this feeling. And just observe it, if necessary through the rest of the day without trying to understand it. It may have the same effect.

Living Joyously

Barry Long has a slightly more long drawn approach to living joyously. He writes:

You are dissipating your energy out into existence through the personality, instead of using it to stay in your reality. The mask is kept on by energy going out. As you deny the projection of the personality, you conserve energy. When enough energy is retained, the mask collapses. It loses its independent and selfish existence. I'm going to show you where you're wasting this energy. Since you will then be conscious of it because you've seen it in your own experience, you'll begin to stop the leakage.

You'll have more energy to address other wasteful

mannerisms, attitudes and behavior. Gradually you'll become more conscious, more responsible, more authentic. Your character will reveal itself and your personality will be less in control of your life.

Anger arises because you are not getting your own way. I am going to mention several things to do or stop doing. They will conserve your energy. To begin with, it will be a challenge. As you get deeper into the process, you may become confused. The personality will always be trying to bamboozle you and make you give up. But keep going: the six exercises will always be there to remind you and guide you. Your own undeniable experience that it's working will be the demonstration of the truth. You will notice that you are lighter, easier, more joyous. A new harmony will start pervading your whole life, within and without.

Stop talking about the past

The personality lives off the past and feeds off you telling your story. Each time you hear yourself indulging in talking about the past, stop. The more you practice, the easier it gets. You may lose some friends who'll say you're getting dull and losing your former interesting and stimulating personality. You'll know by this that you're doing well.

There will be times when you have to refer to the past. However, to break the old habit, initially you must be extreme. The extremity is to not say anything that refers to the past. This includes what happened a minute ago, unless there's a purely practical reason for speaking, such as 'Did you post that letter?'

Don't tell your sad, sad story.

By stopping talking about the past you will eventually stop thinking about the past. And that will be the beginning of the end of worry.

Be true to the situation

Be true to the situation and not to your personal likes

and dislikes. The personality lives off emotional swings—between what you like and what you don't like. It uses the dynamic of the pendulum to keep itself going.

You can't be sure of your likes and dislikes. They change with experience and the years. So be true to the situation, to the event or circumstance you're facing.

What does the situation require? It may not be what suits you personally. For example, if you're employed to do a job, be true to what you're paid for, not to whether you like it or don't like it. If you insist on reacting in dislike, be true to the situation and resign, because clearly, you won't be doing a good job. Complaining about your life, and blaming other people and things for your difficulties, is one of the main leakages of energy.

The personality, remember, actually enjoys conflict. It wants you to go on doing a job and not liking it, because then you can complain and emotionalize about it to your friends. This consumes energy which should be used for taking action one way or the other. Either you do the job by giving up your attitude, or you quit. That's being true to the situation. Action always clears deadlocked energy.

Give up your dishonesty

Give up being dishonest to yourself and your life. Any time you're angry, resentful or depressed, it means you are not being honest: you are not facing life as it is. Anger arises because you are not getting your own way. Instead of being angry, you should be looking at what practical action you can take to get around the obstruction. If there's no practical action you can take, your desire is impractical at this time. To be honest you must face the fact and give up your wanting. Remember, the mask of your personality is dishonesty itself. It hides the fact that if you have a very exciting experience today, you're likely to undergo depression in a couple of days. The personality gets its satisfaction both ways; and you pay for it.

Don't talk unless you've got something to say

The personality is always talking. Talking consumes enormous energy. So this exercise is focused on learning to talk less. 'Talking' refers to talking about something, having a discussion, giving your opinions, speculating, rationalizing and repeating what you've heard. In this exercise, you learn the difference between talking and speaking.

For instance, everyone talks about what the politicians should do. You can't talk about what the politicians should do unless you do something yourself towards righting the situation: write to the politicians, phone them or cast your vote. Then you'll be taking action and be able to speak from your own experience. Otherwise you're just a talker. Only action, or speaking what you live, is true.

No more complaining and blaming

Complaining about your life, and blaming other people and things for your difficulties, is one of the main leakages of energy. When you hear yourself doing this, stop. The truth is that you are responsible for your life. If you're not responsible, it's not your life; and that's absurd. Similarly, if you blame something else for what happens to you, you're giving up responsibility by giving it to others. To be responsible is to be responsible for everything that happens to you, unfolding as your life.

Indeed, there are continual difficulties you have to face. They may seem to have been caused by other agencies. But you have to do your best to sort them out. That's life. You don't complain when you get a promotion at work, do you? You don't blame the boss. You feel you deserved it; that you must have earned it. In other words, you accept that you were responsible. So how can you duck out from being responsible for the not-so-good things that happen to you?

Again, it's the personality being two-faced, not being straight. It presents life as it is not, and gets away with it while you continue to blame and complain.

Tackle habitual small talk

Remember that the personality depends on habitual unconsciousness. Stop the conversational habit of using expressions like darling, honey, my love, and my dear when addressing your partner, friends or casual contacts. If anything, use the person's correct name. After you've broken the habit, you'll find the endearing expression occurs naturally and appropriately. But to begin with, to break the habit and make the situation conscious, don't use such terms.

Don't pat your partner down with silky words and actions when you know you're planning to be dishonest, or you've done something they don't like. Instead, say 'I'm moved to pat you down because I don't want you to react to what I've done or what I'm about to do'. Then tell them straight out what you've done or what you're about to do. Mostly you'll find that you won't do what you were going to do or you'll just do it and cop the force of their disapproval. At least you'll be honest; and such honesty loosens the mask.

Common Expressions

Don't say: 'What I mean is' and 'You know?' or any similar fill-in phrase. These are all unconscious in-words of the western personality, now globally habitual. And don't say 'To be honest' because that implies you're about to be dishonest, or that you're usually a liar. Such phrases have no real meaning and are actually the mask talking.

Practise these exercises in your daily life over the next twelve months or so, and you'll slowly separate from the domination of the personality.

More Dismantling

Now here's an intelligence test. Please ask yourself this question: Do I want to be with, live with, or love somebody who's always moody, angry,restless, sullen, resentful or depressed? If the answer is 'no', then the next question is: Why do I believe that anyone would want to live with me while I have those emotions? As you dismantle the personality and become more one with life, you will start to feel some disintegration of yourself.

You will feel at times you are 'nothing', and that you're losing your identity. Know that it's your personality you're losing, not your identity. Nothing you are or have will disappear. All that goes is the attachment, the identification with the things the personality calls 'me and mine'. And that includes your most intimate and treasured notions of what life and love are about. For in the end, I realize that nothing is 'mine', not even my own body. I am behind it all—the being behind the mask in the bathroom mirror. I am the end of the masquerade.

The Joy Within

Life is to be enjoyed, to be made conscious by enjoying it. For joy is consciousness. When you enjoy anything you do, you are conscious. If you enjoy dancing, you're conscious while dancing. If you enjoy gardening, you're conscious while gardening. If you enjoy your work, you're conscious while working. Enjoy every moment of your life and you're living consciously as well as joyously. It's as simple as that.

Joy or consciousness is your natural state. It's always there. It's like the sun that is always shining above the shadow of the earth and clouds. Stop living in your own shadow, and the sun, the joy, immediately shines. Nothing positive can be done to find joy. It's the practice of negation, shedding the shadow, that does it. Living joyously is the joy of clarit —no problems. My whole life is then a joy or clarity of being—a being of joy and clarity. This is there now, inside you, just waiting to be lived. You don't have to strive for it, search for it or make it. It's you. It's yours, your very being.

Conclusion

From the points of view expressed in the preceding pages on Krishnamurti, it is evident that there can be no end to the ongoing debate on Krishnamurti and his significance to posterity. The debate is itself in the field of thought and therefore irrelevant from Krishnamurti's own viewpoint as are the questions whether he is the genuine world teacher, whether "the process" represents the rising of the Kundalini. There can be no doubt about Krishnamurti's continuing influence. The book *Krishnamurti – 100 Years* by Evelyne Blau provides enough evidence of the number and caliber of the people so influenced. Most of the impact on his audiences and readers is likely to have been more unconscious than conscious as many perceptual processes are. Their unconscious drew them again and again to Krishnamurti's talks and books, even if in the end they thought they understood little. If the conditioning process can be unconscious, so, perhaps, can the deconditioning process. It is possible, and even likely that others will develop more efficient transformative approaches than Krishnamurti's. Some have been outlined in the previous chapter. He may have underestimated the difficulties on the way, but he certainly made it easier for others to trek the same terrain. His success lies chiefly in that.

Index

H

I

J

K

L

M

N

O